Frontiers Of Faith

The Story of
Charles C. & Florence Personeus,
Pioneer Missionaries to Alaska,
"The Last Frontier"
1917-1982

By

AnnaLee Conti

ISBN: 0-7596-8899-0

This book is printed on acid free paper.

All scriptures are taken from the *New King James Version* of the Bible. © Copyright 1979, 1980, 1982, Thomas Nelson, Inc., Publishers.

1stBooks - rev. 04/06/02

TABLE OF CONTENTS

PREFACE

America has always had a frontier. Frontiers have shaped our attitudes. If things didn't work out where we were, we could always go west. Alaska has been called America's "Last Frontier." Where do we go from there? Space challenges us as a new frontier. Men have even walked on the moon. As a frontier, space seems endless, but that frontier is only open to a select few.

One frontier, however, is open to everyone–the frontier of faith. New frontiers of faith open daily to be explored and conquered. This true pioneering experience is available for each one who is not content with the mundane but wants to keep exploring the depths of Christ. You will never run out of frontiers of faith in your lifetime, because God is infinite.

Two people who have done more to shape my faith and challenge me to explore the frontiers of my faith were my maternal grandparents, Charles C. and Florence L. Personeus, pioneer Assemblies of God missionaries to Alaska from 1917 to 1982. In these pages I want to introduce you to my grandparents, their walk of faith, the lessons they learned, the challenges they faced. Just as these two pioneers of faith challenged me to explore the frontiers of my faith, I hope you will be challenged to do the same.

I first knew I would write this book when I was working in an editorial capacity at Assemblies of God Headquarters in Springfield, Missouri, in 1973. My grandparents were visiting us, and Grandma placed a packet in my hands, saying, "Many people have asked me to write our story, but I'm too old to see it through by myself. So I'm placing all my written accounts in your hands to do with as you think best." (Before she died in 1985, I was able to read the rough draft of this book to her and Grandpa.)

Grandma enriched my childhood with her wonderful storytelling, keeping everyone spellbound with her vivid descriptions of their early days in Alaska. As I began to read through her written accounts, I discovered a wealth of material richer than the Alaska-Juneau Gold Mine, which produced over three billion dollars' worth of gold at today's prices. But how could I best tell their story? I began looking for a recurring theme in the Personeuses' lives. And it wasn't hard to find.

The one thing that stood out in all their experiences was their simple, childlike faith in taking God at His Word, especially in the area of divine healing. At the age of 87 Grandma had written, "I have never taken an aspirin in my life. I have found that prayer works better every time." And she wrote from firsthand experiences of many serious illnesses and injuries. Her statement demonstrates the quality of their faith. It was more than mere words; it was faith in action.

As I studied their accounts of healing and living by faith, I began to see the lessons God had taught them through their experiences. I recognized principles that could perhaps be of help to others who are seeking to walk by faith. Through their stories I hope to pass on to you some of these principles for exploring and conquering the frontiers of your faith, as I introduce to you two of God's faithful people, who pioneered the Assemblies of God in Alaska, America's "Last Frontier."

In 1917, when the Personeuses first joined the newly formed General Council of the Assemblies of God, Eudorus N. Bell, one of the early leaders, asked, "When you get to Alaska and find it hard, cold, and discouraging, will you stick?"

"We'll stick," they replied.

And "stick" they did. Long after those early leaders had gone on to their eternal reward, the Personeuses ministered faithfully in Alaska for 65 years. In that time they saw the Assemblies of God in Alaska grow from one struggling mission work in Juneau to more than 80 established churches and mission stations from Ketchikan to Barrow.

Their testimony is presented here, not to gain any personal glory, but that all the glory might go to our wonderful Lord and Savior Jesus Christ, who was faithful to meet their every need. I'm sure they would add their "Amen" to my prayer that through this book you might profit by their experiences and come to know the God they served so faithfully.

And I hope you enjoy their story.

AnnaLee Conti

CHAPTER 1

ALASKA CALL

"I heard the voice of the Lord saying, Whom shall I send, and who will go for us? Then said I, Here am I; send me" (Isaiah 6:8).

Carl watched helplessly as his young wife, wearing multiple layers of clothes, huddled on the table, her booted feet propped on top of the Yukon stove. The Taku wind prowled around their tiny shack like the Big Bad Wolf trying to huff and puff their walls in. As each icy breath blasted the cabin, threatening to dislodge it from its precarious perch on the side of Mt. Roberts, a fine powder of snow sifted through the cracks between the bare boards. Balls of frost marked the location of each nail head. That morning he had broken his pocketknife trying to chip away the ice from around the door, so he could go out to the post office. Now it had refrozen.

He could see his wife taking shallow breaths to avoid inhaling the acrid cigar smoke that wafted through the cheesecloth tacked to rough boards and covered with wallpaper that divided their one-room apartment from the other rooms in the cabin. Located up a long "street" of wooden stairs called Decker Way, just up from South Franklin Street (then called Front Street) in 1917 Juneau, it had been the only place they could afford.

How could I have brought my wife to this place? he thought. *How have our lives come to this? I thought I heard God's call to be a missionary to Alaska. Could I have been wrong?*

Alaska—Land of Ice and Snow...Seward's Icebox...Seward's Folly...Land of the Eskimos...Igloos...Gold Rush. These are things the name "Alaska" evoked in people's minds at the turn of the Twentieth Century. But Carl knew God saw people lost in darkness, rushing pell mell into hell—people for whom His Son died. And when God wants to reach out with the Gospel of His love, He calls a man. Carl had been so sure he was that man.

In his mind he began rehearsing the events in his life that had led him to this place...

On January 13, 1888, a baby boy was born in a Methodist parsonage at Masonville, New York (just north of Binghamton). Charles Cardwell Personeus was the third of seven children born to Charles Byron Personeus, also the son of a Methodist minister, and his wife, Flora Ellis. Since his father's name was Charles, and the name Cardwell seemed too cumbersome to be attached to the little fellow, his parents called him "Carl," as he was known all his life to his family and friends. Carl was quite rambunctious as a baby and loved to throw his bottle out of his carriage. One time he threw it out and decided to jump out after it, landing on his head in the broken glass. His mother had to stitch up a deep cut with needle and thread, and he bore the scar just above his right temple at the hairline as long as he lived.

Throughout Carl's childhood, the Methodist Church moved the growing family from town to town and parsonage to parsonage every two years, and every two years a new little one was added to the family. Little Byron and John, however, died in infancy. As Carl grew older, he helped the family financially by doing odd jobs, such as stoking the neighbor's furnace and shoveling snow. He also had a paper route, which meant he had to get up at four o'clock in the morning to deliver all the papers before school. Carl's father and aunt were excellent musicians on the piano and organ. His aunt offered to give Carl piano lessons, but he refused, not wanting to sit still and practice. He lived to regret that boyish decision.

When Carl was eleven years old, he and his older brother Edgar visited a Baptist church, where Carl went to the altar to accept Christ as his personal Savior. "But I didn't really live the Christian life," Carl recalled. However, at the age of thirteen he joined the Methodist Church.

The next year, Carl's father became interested in John Alexander Dowie, who was known for his success in praying for the sick. In 1900, Dowie had organized his followers and planned a Christian community called Zion City, near Chicago, Illinois. When Dowie's financial mismanagement and excesses became known, Carl's father left Dowie-ism and joined A. B. Simpson's Christian and Missionary Alliance (CMA). Not being allowed to baptize by immersion and understanding that divine healing is provided for in the Atonement, but not being allowed to preach it, he felt he no longer belonged in the Methodist Church.

In 1903, Carl's father assumed the pastorate of a CMA church in Binghamton. That July, his father contracted a severe case of pleurisy. At the bedside of his deathly ill father, Carl, now fifteen, renewed his commitment to Jesus Christ.

After four weeks of grave illness, Carl's father told the family one morning, "Warm up the house. The Lord told me I should get up today." He arose from his sickbed and walked four miles to a prayer meeting. Then he visited another home where he sang and played the piano.

The next year, Carl's father was invited to hold meetings in Bridgeport, Connecticut. On April 17, 1905, he moved his family there so he could assume the pastorate of the mission he had started in Bridgeport.

At about this same time, young Carl began to feel God's call upon his life. He thought perhaps God was calling him to be a missionary in China.

Then, on July 27, 1905, Charles Byron Personeus died suddenly of an acute respiratory infection, just one week after his forty-eighth birthday. After his father's death, 17-year-old Carl had to quit school and go to work in a button factory to help support his mother and the younger children, as well as look after the mission his father had started. The next year, he went to work in a print shop, where he worked seven years and learned the printing trade.

In July 1908, Carl attended a CMA convention at Nyack, New York. There, he heard about the baptism in the Holy Spirit, as evidenced by speaking in other tongues, and he began to seek his own Baptism. At that time, he was actively involved in the CMA church in Bridgeport, Connecticut, as the Sunday school superintendent and missions treasurer. During special meetings at that church, however, when a visiting evangelist began to preach about the Pentecostal experience, the pastor promptly stopped him.

Carl, who played the trombone, had organized a mission band and had been distributing tracts in saloons, so he started a rescue mission to disciple the new converts. He still retained his membership in the CMA, but his mission work gradually expanded until he became its first superintendent in January 1910.

Carl's usual practice was to arrange for someone to preach in each service. About a month after becoming superintendent of the mission, the Lord asked Carl, "Will you trust Me to provide the speaker for the service next Sunday afternoon?"

"Certainly, Lord. I'll trust You." So Carl did not arrange for a preacher for the next week.

When the time came to start that service, however, no speaker had arrived. Undaunted, though a little nervous, Carl faithfully called out the number for the opening hymn. He was in mid-sentence when the door opened quietly, and a lady slipped in.

"There is your preacher," the Lord seemed to say to Carl.

Believing God had arranged this service, he obediently walked to where the lady was sitting and asked her to preach in the service. She was about to refuse because of the short notice, she told him later, but the Lord impressed on her the words of Psalm 102:13, "You will arise and have mercy on Zion; for the time to favor her, yes, the set time, has come." Thinking on these words, she could not refuse to speak.

The lady was Alice Belle Garrigus, who later left a life of relative ease and comfort in the United States to take the Pentecostal message to Newfoundland.

That afternoon she preached God's message for the hour. The mission work had been so discouraging that those in charge had decided that unless something unusual took place, this would be the last meeting, and the mission would be closed.

When the service ended, one man, who had supported the mission financially, went to Miss Garrigus and said, "I asked the Lord to give me a crumb today, and I got a loaf."

The discouraged believers decided that a week of special services would be conducted. And they were indeed special! Carl Personeus received the baptism in the Holy Spirit, with the initial physical evidence of speaking in other tongues as the Spirit gave him the utterance, and Miss Garrigus later described him as "a young giant filled with new wine." Thus, Carl's rescue mission became the first Pentecostal mission in Bridgeport, Connecticut.

That July, a lady evangelist was ministering at the mission. In the course of her message she said, "I believe the Lord wants to call someone to the mission field tonight."

Silently, Carl prayed, "Lord, is it I?"

Immediately, the Lord spoke to his heart, "Alaska."

Carl knew very little about Alaska, but he responded, "Yes, Lord, if You want me to go to Alaska, I'll go."

Two years later as Carl listened to a missionary from the West Indies, he prayed, "Lord, should I go to the West Indies?"

The Lord spoke to his heart again, "Alaska is the field to which I have called you."

Finally, in 1913, Carl's younger sister Ruth was able to assume the care of their mother, and his older brother Edgar was willing to take charge of the mission, thus freeing him to pursue his missionary call. (Edgar later went to Liberia as a missionary. When he had to return to the States after four years because of his health, he taught at Bethel Bible School in Newark, New Jersey. Their sister, Mattie, served forty years as an Assemblies of God missionary in India near the border of Nepal.)

Although he had been preaching for eight years, Carl felt he needed more study to prepare himself for missionary service, so he applied for admission to the Rochester Bible Training School in Rochester, New York. He entered Bible school in October 1913, at the age of 25. During the summer vacation of 1914, he and Jacob Mueller, another student who later went to India, held evangelistic meetings together in Upstate New York.

After his graduation and ordination in the spring of 1915, Carl felt he was ready to go to Alaska, but the Lord instructed him to stay at the Bible school. For another two years he remained at the school as the Dean of Men and head printer in the school's printing office. He also assisted in holding services in several nearby communities during those years.

Meanwhile, the Lord had been preparing a bride for Charles C. ("Carl") Personeus.

CHAPTER 2

FORSAKING ALL

"They forsook all, and followed him" (Luke 5:11).

On November 3, 1888, (only 10 months after the birth of Charles Cardwell Personeus) Florence Evelyn LeFevre was born near Strasburg, Pennsylvania, the eighth of 11 children born to a "country gentleman," George Newton LeFevre, and his wife Laura Long. They lived in a stately 27-room mansion on five square miles of land deeded to the LeFevre ancestors by William Penn.

The LeFevre ancestors were French Huguenots who had been severely persecuted for their faith. Isaac LeFevre, at age 16, was the lone survivor when his family was massacred for their Protestant faith in Strasburg, France, in 1685, after the revocation of the Edict of Nantes. He escaped with nothing but the family Bible his mother had baked in a loaf of bread. (That Bible, printed in Geneva in 1608, is now in the vault in the library of the Lancaster County Historical Society, Lancaster, Pennsylvania, and may be viewed upon request.) Seeking freedom to worship God, Isaac eventually came to America, by way of Bavaria, Holland, and England, with the Ferree family, of the French nobility, who were also Huguenots. In 1712, they had obtained a deed from William Penn for land in Lancaster County. Isaac married the Ferree's daughter Catherine, and the family sailed to America to claim their land. These first white settlers in Lancaster County, finding the religious freedom they were seeking, named their little settlement "Paradise." A monument to them stands today by the railroad tracks on the outskirts of Paradise, Pennsylvania.

Florence was born to be a lady. The family had a rich ancestral heritage. Her mother, Laura Long LeFevre, was a descendant of Alexander Hamilton, the first Secretary of the Treasury of the United States. Both George and Laura were university graduates. George had great plans for his large family. He wanted his children to marry the ones he chose for them and settle down in Lancaster County around his farm and establish "LeFevreville" on the land William Penn had deeded to their ancestors.

A strict disciplinarian, he believed all children should work hard and his were no exception. Since he would not allow them to associate with the Amish or the Pennsylvania Dutch children who lived around them, the children sought companionship among themselves. Florence became an avid reader, and the LeFevre home was well supplied with excellent literature. Often, her younger brothers and sisters would coax Florence to read aloud to them while they did her chores as well as their own.

So concerned was he for the cultural advancement of his children, George LeFevre brought many distinguished visitors into his home. He would throw lawn parties to which professors and other distinguished guests from Philadelphia were invited, but never any of their country neighbors. One such guest George brought home with him from one of his frequent business trips to Philadelphia was George Sherman, a veteran missionary to China. This man's visit opened a whole new world to them. Seeing such a large family of bright young adults and teenagers, he immediately began to encourage all of them to become missionaries. As a result of that visit, four of the LeFevre children would become missionaries, serving a combined total of more than 150 years on foreign fields.

George LeFevre was outraged! As each of the older children left home to follow God's leading in their lives, he disowned and disinherited them. He forbade the other members of the family to even mention their names in his presence. Hoping to persuade them to return home, he piled extra work on the younger children, even some which had been done by hired hands, so the older ones would see that their leaving was causing hardships on their brothers and sisters. Yet, one by one, they left. The missionary flame, having been kindled, only burned brighter.

Florence's eldest sister, Anna, went to Nyack Bible Institute, where she worked her way through school doing housework for Dr. A. B. Simpson, founder of the Christian and Missionary Alliance. In his living room Anna received the baptism in the Holy Spirit as evidenced by the initial physical evidence of speaking in tongues. When she graduated, she went to Chile, South America, where she spent 40 years as a missionary.

Mary left home to work for the Lord wherever the door was opened for her. Laura Zenobia, nicknamed "Birdie" for her bright, sunny disposition, took a position as associate editor of *The Sunday School Times*, a weekly Christian magazine. Later, she wrote nine Christian novels published under the pen name "Zenobia Bird." Charles attended

Moody Bible Institute in Chicago; then he too spent 40 years in Chile as a missionary.

Although she loved school, Florence was not allowed to attend high school. Her father stopped her schooling, hoping to shame the older children into leaving their fields of Christian service when they saw the effect of their actions on Florence.

The LeFevre home contained a large library. "You read these books," George LeFevre told Florence, "and you'll get a better education than you could get in high school."

Florence did learn the printing trade from her father, who was a lawyer, historian, editor and publisher of a weekly newspaper, *The Home*, and the Lord used that knowledge to work out His purpose in her life.

The newspaper print shop was located at the back of the house. There, Florence spent many hours setting type and running the printing press. Each week on the night before the countywide weekly was to be mailed, the children would have to stay up all night to fold, wrap, and address the papers because the older children had left home. Ironically, the subtitle of *The Home* read, "The Life of the Nation, the Strength of the Church, and the Purity of Society depend upon the Intelligent and Well ordered Homes of the People." George LeFevre prided himself on being a righteous man. In *The Home* he actively campaigned for Prohibition. And he was one of the first Americans to translate the New Testament into English from the original Greek. Yet, where his family was concerned, he wanted total domination, even to the point of denying the call of God on their lives.

The hardships and heartaches soon caused Florence to become very bitter against her father. Yet, she had a fun loving and imaginative nature. She frequently entertained her younger brothers and sister with fantastic stories.

Florence's parents were strict Baptists, but the children were allowed to attend other churches from time to time. On January 31, 1904, her older brother Charles led Florence, who was 15, into a real born again experience. They had been attending a Methodist revival. That Sunday afternoon Charles overheard her telling one of her fantastic stories to the younger children.

"Would you like to say all those things in front of God?" Charles asked her.

"No," she gulped, aghast at the thought.

When Charles began to talk with her further about her soul, she grew rebellious and ran and locked herself in a closet. Following her, Charles talked with her through the locked door until she finally broke down and gave her life to Jesus. He then gave her several verses to claim as promises. One, in particular, was to become especially meaningful to the shy teenage girl: "So we may boldly say, The Lord is my helper; I will not fear. What can man do to me?" (Hebrews 13:6). Although she still struggled with bitterness against her father, she now had Someone to help her.

Two years later, Florence attended an old-fashioned Christian and Missionary Alliance camp meeting. One Sunday, several foreign missionaries spoke, telling of the need for more workers to carry the Gospel to the lost. Then Dr. A. B. Simpson arose and asked, "How many of you would be willing to go if God called you?"

An awed hush gripped the congregation. Florence sat with her head bowed in prayer, pondering the question. She thought of her home and her loved ones. "Lord, do you want *me* to leave all for Thee?" she cried silently.

Then the Lord spoke to her heart: "You did not chose Me, but I chose you, and appointed you, that you should go and bear fruit" (John 15:16). "He that loves father or mother more than Me is not worthy of Me" (Matthew 10:37). Then she remembered, "And everyone who has left houses or brothers or sisters or father or mother, ...for My name's sake, shall receive a hundredfold, and everlasting life" (Matthew 19:29).

With her eyes closed in prayer, she stood to her feet with the other young people who were consecrating their lives to the Lord's work. She didn't know how or where the Lord was leading her, although she wanted to go to Chile, where her older sister and brother had gone. But she knew the Lord had called her to dedicate her life to His service, and she had answered, "Yes, Lord, I'll go where You want me to go."

After that commitment, it seemed to her that the trials of her life increased, and her burdens grew heavier. She couldn't understand why, yet deep within her soul she felt peace and joy greater than ever before. Life would have been unbearable if it had not been for the love of her Savior and of the other members of her family. During her teens she often visited an elderly lady, Mrs. Ella J. Winter, who would pray with her and encourage her to stay close to Jesus. One time, Mrs. Winter gave Florence a little poem that began, "Child of my love, lean hard." Florence felt the Lord was telling her through that poem that every trial and heartache were part of His training in her life preparing her for His service.

Her father bitterly opposed any of his children who wanted to be missionaries, and he did everything he could to discourage them. After her commitment to the Lord, Florence was no longer allowed to attend camp meetings or missionary services. Neither would her father allow her to be baptized in water, so she promised the Lord she would be baptized as soon as she turned 21. But when she passed her twenty-first birthday, she still did not follow the Lord in baptism. She was so timid and afraid of facing the world alone, she dreaded making the break and leaving her home, knowing she would never be allowed to return.

As Florence struggled with the decision to leave home, she found this poem written by George MacDonald and copied it into her notebook, which she titled, "Stepping Stones in My Life in the Straight and Narrow Way."

WHAT CHRIST SAID

I said, "Let me walk in the field,"
He said, "No, walk in the town."
I said, "There are no flowers there."
He said, "No flowers; but a crown."

I said, "But the skies are black,
There is nothing but noise and din."
And He wept as He sent me back.
"There is more," He said, "there is sin."

I said, "But the air is thick,
And the fogs are veiling the sun."
He answered, "Yet souls are sick,
And souls in the dark undone."

I said, "I will miss the light,
And friends will miss me, they say."
He answered, "Choose tonight
If I am to miss you, or they."

I pleaded for time to be given.
He said, "Is it so hard to decide?
It will not seem hard in heaven,
To have followed the steps of your guide."

I cast one look at the fields
And set my face to the town.
He said, "My child, do you yield?
Will you leave the flowers for the crown?"

Then into His hand went mine,
And into my heart came He,
And I walk in the light divine
The path that I had feared to see.

—George MacDonald

As she struggled, Florence felt miserable. Having such a strict, harsh father had distorted her understanding of God. Feeling she had committed the unpardonable sin by not being baptized as soon as she turned 21 as she had promised God, she felt God had forsaken her. She wanted to talk to her brother Charles. But Charles, who was home on furlough from Chile, was not allowed to visit their home because he had become a missionary.

Florence had a cousin, Actin, who owned a drugstore in nearby Lancaster. She knew he had helped her sisters Anna and Birdie, as well as Charles, after they had been banished from their home. So Florence contacted Actin, asking him to arrange for her to see Charles at the drugstore. After she had poured out her agony of feeling she had committed the unpardonable sin, Charles reassured her that she had not. When they had prayed together, she felt much better.

As Florence left the drugstore and ran across the street to catch the trolley home, she did not see the bobsled racing down the street toward her. It hit her, tossing her into the air like a rag doll. She landed on her head and sprawled unconscious in the snowy street. Passersby rushed to her aid. Someone had seen her leave Actin's drugstore, so they carried her inside. Actin bandaged her bleeding head and cared for her until she felt better, in time to catch the next trolley.

When she alighted from the trolley at her destination, Mr. Chandler, a friend of the family, who worked nearby, saw her. Seeing her bandaged head, he asked, "What happened to you?"

When Florence explained about her accident, Mr. Chandler was indignant. "Your father and Lincoln [Florence's eldest brother] were on that trolley! I was here when they got off it. You mean to tell me they left you to be cared for by strangers? They didn't even get off to find out if you were dead or alive? What kind of father is he?"

The wound to her heart hurt more than the bump on her head. She realized her father must have seen her come out of Cousin Actin's drugstore where he had forbidden his children to go. Angry with her, he had even forbidden Lincoln to help her.

(I should tell you that Grandma never talked about this incident. Her own daughter had never even heard of it. When Grandma was 92 and I had completed my first rough draft of this book, I was reading it aloud to her. In her written accounts she had referred to this incident only as "an accident that could have taken my life." I asked her for more details, and she reluctantly told me this story. At first, she asked me not to include it in this book. Feeling it was crucial to helping the readers understand the kind of persecution she had to overcome, I persuaded her to allow me to write it. Although Grandma was quite a storyteller, I feel the story she didn't tell reveals more about her character than any story she ever told. Why didn't she want this story told? She loved her father and didn't want to bring shame to him or to the family. She always lived by the motto: "If you can't say something nice about someone, don't say anything at all." Remembering that incident was extremely painful. She knew that talking about it would only feed the hurt and would drive it into her spirit, so she kept quiet about it.)

As Florence trudged slowly home that day, the Lord spoke to her again, "Do you want to please your earthly father, or do the will of your Heavenly Father and Jesus who died for you and called you to follow Him?"

She knew she must take the steps that would lead to separation from her parents, her brothers and sisters, her home. Her father had warned her that she would be disowned, disinherited, and could never return home if she left. Yet, as she made her decision, she felt peace in her soul and the assurance that Jesus would never leave her nor forsake her. Still, she knew it would be hard to leave her family and the beautiful 27-room home, which she had loved since infancy, knowing she could never come back again.

When Florence encountered her mother as she arrived home, she told her, "I'll be the next one to leave home."

And she went to her room to begin packing. Her father intercepted her. Not even asking how she was, he began to lecture her about children obeying their parents.

Florence had always dreamed of being a nurse like Florence Nightingale, for whom she had been named, so Mr. Chandler's daughter helped her get into nurse's training. First, she had to take her high school equivalency test, on which she scored a high grade. Then she entered the West Chester Hospital at West Chester, Pennsylvania, to begin training as a nurse. However, after several months she had to leave because she wasn't strong enough physically. The head nurse told her to go home, but Florence couldn't go home!

Staying with relatives, she found work in a shirt factory, but she could not make enough money to live on, let alone save for Bible school. People began telling her she could never be a missionary. "You're not strong enough. No church would accept you as a missionary," they said. She was homesick, lonely, and very discouraged. Doubts that God had called her robbed her of the peace she had had when she left home. Miserable and discouraged, she was tempted to end it all.

Huddled in a heap on the floor in a cloakroom of the shirt factory one day, battling with sickness and despair, Florence cried out to God for help. "Please give me the peace and assurance I once had," she pleaded. Then the Lord reminded her that she had not yet been baptized in water.

"I'll be baptized at the first opportunity, Lord," she promised.

And once again God spoke to her heart. "Will you go to the Northwest?"

Happy to hear His voice again, she sobbed, "Yes, Lord, anywhere! Only give me your peace again!" It was then that the Lord assured her that she would go to Bible school.

Having promised the Lord to be baptized at her first opportunity, she decided to attend a Christian and Missionary Alliance camp meeting so she could be baptized. On the train foul mouthed girls from the shirt factory made fun of her, but nothing could deter her. The baptism was to be conducted in the Conestoga River. When Florence saw the waters of the river, made very muddy by heavy rains, she wondered how she would ever get her long blonde hair clean again. But she determined to be baptized anyway. As she came up out of those muddy waters, the glory of the Lord and His peace that passes all understanding thrilled her soul as never before.

Florence soon quit her job at the shirt factory because a position nursing an invalid had opened up for her. She found herself among congenial, but worldly, friends who wanted her to go with them to their worldly amusements. She enjoyed having kind friends and didn't want to offend them when they wanted her to do things she had been taught were not right for a Christian, things which did not glorify God, so she began to compromise. Once again, she lost the joy of the Lord, which truly was proving to be her strength.

But God did not allow her to drift with the tide of worldly companions too long. One evening as she was learning to play cards, she felt as though someone had jerked her hand back as she reached out to take cards. Immediately, she realized the Lord didn't want her to play cards, so she excused herself. As she left, she overheard one girl say, "Oh, that little Puritan! She makes me sick!"

Another time, one of the fellows wanted to teach her to dance. As she stepped out on the dance floor and her partner began to show her the steps, she felt as though someone had thrust a rod down her spine, and she stiffened up as though rigor mortis had set in.

"Loosen up," her partner encouraged.

"I can't. Dancing is just not for me," she replied as she left the dance.

Another poem Florence wrote in her journal, "Stepping Stones in My Life in the Straight and Narrow," seems to describe her struggle during this period of her life. The author is not identified. Perhaps Florence, a poet herself, wrote it.

THE ANSWERED PRAYER

She asked to be made like her Savior,
He took her then at her word,
And sent her a heart crushing burden,
Till the depths of her soul was stirred.

14

She asked for a faith, strong, yet simple.
He permitted the dark clouds to come,
And she staggered by faith through the darkness
For the storm quite obscured the sun.

She prayed to be filled with a passion
Of love for lost souls and for God,
And again in response to her longings,
She sank 'neath the chastening rod.

She wanted a place in His vineyard,
He took her away from her home,
And placed her among hardened sinners
Where she humanly stood, all alone.

She saw she must give up ambitions
Which had been her "air castles" for years,
But, as she knelt in consecration,
She whispered, "Amen," through her tears.

She wanted a meek, lowly spirit—
The work He gave answered that cry,
Till some who had once been companions,
With a pitying smile passed her by.

She asked to lean hard on her Savior,
He took human props quite away,
Till no earthly friend could give comfort,
And she could do nothing but pray.

I saw her go out in the vineyard
To harvest the ripening grain;
Her eyes were still moistened with weeping,
Her heart was yet throbbing with pain.

> But many a heart that was broken
> And many a wrecked, blighted life
> Were made to thank God for her coming
> And rejoiced in the midst of the strife.
>
> She had prayed to be made like the Savior
> And the burdens He gave her to bear
> Had been but the great Sculptor's teaching
> To help answer her earnest prayer.

Once again, Florence knew she must find another place to live. Her fear and timidity made meeting strangers torturous. Yet, she longed for spiritual fellowship, so she decided to try to find a Christian home that took in boarders. When asking around if there were any strong Christians living in the neighborhood, one person told her, "The Buchwalters in Paradise are very strong Christians, but I think they have too much religion!"

Florence thought, *Well, that's better than too little*.

But when she looked them up, they told her, "We really don't care to have any boarders, but we'll pray about it." And God spoke to their hearts that they should take her into their home.

Florence soon realized that the Buchwalters were Pentecostal. She knew very little about the baptism in the Holy Spirit. Every evening, the Buchwalters gathered for family worship, which Florence really enjoyed. She felt the power of God in that home as she had never felt it before. As the family prayed together, praising and rejoicing in God's wonderful provisions for His children, she realized there were spiritual blessings she had never known.

A great hunger and longing for more of God filled her soul until she could not keep back the tears as she witnessed the power and joy and victory in them. Ashamed of her tears, Florence would hurry from the room before the family arose from their knees. They thought she was weary of the long seasons of prayer until one evening Ada, one of the daughters (who later went to China as a missionary, married Leonard Bolton, and spent many years in missions), raised her head and saw Florence's tears.

Following her to her room, Ada asked tenderly, "Florence, what's wrong?"

"I don't know," Florence sobbed. "I've been a Christian for years, but you have something I've never known."

"Praise the Lord!" Ada responded. "I've been wanting to tell you about it, but you were so reserved and quiet, I didn't know if you'd care to listen. It's the baptism in the Holy Spirit that makes the difference."

And she went on to explain about this wonderful experience as described in Acts Chapter 2. Thus, Florence began to seek for the infilling of the Holy Spirit for herself.

Florence, however, was still not ready to meet her future husband. God had another hard lesson to teach her.

CHAPTER 3

HE'S STILL THE SAME TODAY

"Jesus Christ is the same yesterday, today, and forever" (Hebrews 13:8).

For the next several years Florence experienced very poor health. Often she could scarcely eat. Her right arm and hand were aflame with raw, itchy eczema. She had gone from one doctor to another, seeking relief, but no one had been able to help her.

One day in 1914, when she arrived home from the Park Seed Company where she now worked printing their catalogs, she found the Buchwalters all excited.

"Mrs. Maria B. Woodworth-Etter, a lady evangelist, is starting special meetings in a big tent in Philadelphia," Ada told her. "I'm packing my suitcase to go and hear her."

When she returned home, Ada described the marvelous miracles that were occurring in answer to prayer. Florence was amazed. She had been taught that the day of miracles was past and that now we were supposed to depend on doctors and medicine. Her interest aroused, she decided to travel to Philadelphia to see for herself how God was working those miracles. Timidly, she sat far back in the big tent, straining her ears and eyes to see what was taking place. Mrs. Woodworth-Etter preached the Word of God with power, and Florence sensed the presence of the Lord as many sang in the Spirit.

Not content to remain on the outskirts of God's blessings, Florence began to move nearer to the front in each succeeding service she attended. She saw sick people go forward to be prayed for and leave the platform rejoicing. People were coming from far and near, bringing others to be healed. Mrs. Woodworth-Etter continued to preach the Word with power, encouraging everyone to "Have faith in God." Florence longed to see some of the miracles up close, but the crowds hindered her view.

Then one Monday afternoon the tent was not so crowded, and a number of chairs in the choir were empty. The song leader asked for volunteers to come up and fill the empty seats in the choir.

A lady sitting beside Florence said, "Come on, let's go up and help with the singing."

Feeling shy, Florence answered, "But I don't belong here."

"Well, do you belong to the Lord?" the lady asked.

"Oh, yes!" Florence answered.

"Then come and sing for Him." So Florence followed her up.

As they were seated with the choir, Florence realized with joy and humility the goodness of God. She had wanted to see the miracles up close. Now there she was, sitting just behind Mrs. Woodworth-Etter and the assisting ministers where she could see each one that came for prayer.

Some of the people asked for prayer for nerves, for stomach trouble, for insomnia, and other things not outwardly visible. Then a man with a crippled hand came forward for prayer. The hand resembled a hard, dry lump of bone.

As Florence looked at that hand, she said in her heart, "Lord, if you heal that hand, I'll know the day of miracles is NOT past."

Mrs. Woodworth-Etter and the other ministers anointed the man with a dab of oil on the forehead and prayed. Then one of the ministers commanded in a clear, strong voice, "In the name of Jesus Christ of Nazareth, open your hand!"

They all stepped back to watch as that man slowly opened his hand. Flesh and blood filled the dry skin. He opened and closed his hand several times as though he could scarcely believe his own eyes. Then he shouted, "Glory! I haven't been able to open that hand for years."

He leaped in the air and ran shouting and rejoicing from the platform, while the people shouted praises to the Lord.

And Florence prayed, "Thank you, Lord! Now I KNOW You still work miracles today."

Later, she too asked for prayer. She prayed, "Lord, if You will heal the eczema on my hand and arm which I can see, I will trust You to take care of the rest of my body where I can't see."

Looking back, she wished she had claimed complete deliverance that day. The Lord healed her of the eczema, but her general health continued to deteriorate day after day.

Florence continued to work at the print shop, trying to save enough money to go to Bible school, but it seemed the more she and the

Buchwalters prayed for her healing, the weaker she became. She could scarcely eat or sleep. Finally, too weak to go to work, she kept to her bed.

Those were dark days, but she was learning to say with Job, "Though he slay me, yet will I trust in him." Finally, one night she lost hope, seeing only death ahead for her. Alone with God, she reminded Him of how He had told her to go to Bible school. She thought of the joyful assurance she had felt in her soul when she had received the letter of acceptance to the Bible school the Buchwalters had recommended to her—the Rochester Bible Training School. As she had read that letter, the Lord had assured her, "This is the path for you to take."

Suddenly, as she prayed, God exchanged the passive faith she had held in her heart for active faith.

Her passive faith said, "I believe God *can* do it."

Her active faith now said, "I believe God *will* do it for me right *now*."

She cried out, "Lord, You said I would go to Bible school. Then You will have to heal me."

As she prayed that, she felt life surge through her spirit, soul, and body, bringing warmth to her chilled, weakened limbs. She lay on her bed praising the Lord until she fell into a deep, healthful slumber. When she awoke, she felt strong and refreshed. She dressed, joined the family for breakfast, and then went to work.

When she walked in the door at the print shop, the other printer stared at her in amazement. "I didn't think I'd ever see you walk into this office again!" he exclaimed. "Why, you look like a new girl!"

"I feel like a new girl!" she responded.

All day she just bubbled over with praises to Jesus, her Great Physician. "Jesus *is* the same yesterday, today, and forever!" Now she knew it first hand.

The rest of the summer Florence worked ten hours a day, six days a week in the printing office, then gathered local news from seven till nine in the evenings and wrote it up for a daily newspaper. In those days, however, girls were not paid the same wages as the men received. After she paid all her bills, she had very little money left for Bible school. But she hoped to work in the school's printing office where she knew they printed many tracts, as well as a monthly paper called *Trust*.

Leaving her job to go to Rochester, New York, to Bible school, where she knew no one, took a real act of faith for the shy Florence. She had written to Miss Susan A. Duncan, Director of the Rochester Bible Training School, concerning working in the printing office. Miss Duncan had written back that they had regular printers who did all the printing, but to come anyway and trust the Lord to meet her expenses.

"We have prayed over your letter of application and feel it is the Lord's will for you to come," Miss Duncan wrote.

One evening in early September 1915, the Dean of Men at the Rochester Bible Training School was asked to stay up after hours to greet a new student arriving late that night by train from Pennsylvania. A handsome young man with black hair and blue eyes answered Florence's timid knock.

"Miss LeFevre? I'm Carl Personeus," he said, noting her blonde hair and blue eyes. But Florence couldn't even pronounce his name, let alone remember it.

Shortly after her arrival at the school, Miss Duncan asked Florence, "Are you the young lady who wrote that she was a printer?"

"Why, yes," Florence responded.

"One of our regular printers is leaving unexpectedly, and we'd like you to work two hours a day at the printing office to help pay your expenses," Miss Duncan told her.

"How wonderfully God has worked things out!" Florence exclaimed.

But she didn't yet fully realize just how wonderfully God was working things out! In the print shop she would be working with Carl Personeus.

Just about a month after her arrival at the Bible school, on October 11, 1915, in one of the classrooms, Florence received the baptism in the Holy Spirit for which she had been so hungry. At that time, the Lord reaffirmed her Call to the Northwest and gave her a vision of scenes of a Native village in Alaska, which she later identified as Klukwan, when they actually spent two winters ministering there several years later.

Working in the printing shop together gave Carl and Florence the opportunity to get better acquainted. They soon discovered they shared a common calling. In fact, they were the only ones in the entire school whom God had called to Alaska. Their common interest in Alaska soon led to a romantic interest in each other. Now Carl understood why God had instructed him to remain at the school. On October 14, 1915, Carl asked Florence to marry him, and the couple announced their engagement.

During this time, one thing that greatly puzzled Florence was the return of the eczema. One day at work she told Carl how the Lord had healed her of eczema. "But it looks like it's coming back. What should I do?"

He answered, "If the Lord healed it, then stand on His faithfulness. Praise the Lord for your healing. Don't look at the symptoms. The devil wants to put the eczema back on you. You must resist the devil, believe God, and praise Him for healing you."

At the service that night, Florence gave her testimony and praised God for healing her of eczema. Every symptom disappeared! That lesson in faith taught her that victory comes with persevering praise and thanksgiving.

Wanting to do what was proper, Carl wrote to Florence's father to ask for her hand in marriage. George LeFevre wrote back a lengthy letter, pointing out that if Carl were the gentleman he seemed to be, he would not want to marry his rebellious, disobedient daughter, whom he compared to the Prodigal Son.

Knowing God had planned for their lives to be joined together, Carl and Florence were married in the parlor at the Bible school on April 5, 1916, between Florence's first and second year of Bible school. After a honeymoon trip to Niagara Falls, which according to their journal cost $29.89, they visited relatives in Pennsylvania and Connecticut before returning to Rochester. For the next school year Carl continued to serve as Dean of Men, and Florence became the Dean of Women.

Florence graduated and was ordained to the Full Gospel ministry in April 1917. Both of them were now ready for the ministry to which God had called them.

CHAPTER 4

ALASKA BOUND

"When he brings out his own sheep, he goes before them" (John 10:4).

Florence and Carl were now ready to go to Alaska, but they knew very little about the land of their calling. And no one else seemed to know any more. They could not even find out what their fare to Alaska would cost.

Whenever they mentioned their plans, people would exclaim, "What? Going to Alaska? Why, you'll freeze!" They seemed to think only of Eskimos living in ice igloos.

Shortly after graduation in 1917, the Personeuses attended a missionary meeting. The speaker, a missionary to India, told them, "If you're going to be missionaries to Alaska, you should let people know." He suggested they attend a missionary convention that was to be held in Stormville, New York.

"If you are given an opportunity to speak, tell about your Call to Alaska," he advised.

The Personeuses followed the missionary's suggestion and attended the missionary convention. When he was given the opportunity to speak, Carl was able to talk for less than 10 minutes about Alaska, because he knew so little about that land.

Afterwards, he grumbled to Florence, "I couldn't even talk 10 minutes about Alaska. How can I go there?"

The next day he was still feeling very discouraged about going to Alaska when several other ministers invited him to go with them to the train depot in their Model T Ford. As they approached a railroad crossing, Carl could see a train coming, but the driver seemed to pay no attention to it. Finally, he swerved just in time to avoid being demolished by a thru train. The train, however, passed so close to their automobile that it tore off a section of the Model T right next to Carl's head.

Thoroughly frightened, Carl prayed, "All right, Lord, I'll go!"

The next day, the Personeuses resigned their jobs at the Bible school and began preparations for going to Alaska. August 9, 1917, they left Rochester to visit family and friends in New York, Pennsylvania, New

Jersey, and Connecticut, to say "goodbye," to speak about Alaska, and to gather supplies and a warm wardrobe.

They had only been gone a few days when Carl received a call from the draft board in Rochester to come in and take a physical examination. World War I was raging in Europe, and he was being drafted! Carl passed his physical, but he applied for a ministerial deferment, which was granted. When it is God's time, even Uncle Sam cannot stand in the way!

Knowing nothing more about Alaska at the end of the summer, the Personeuses returned to Rochester for a final farewell. They still did not know what their fares to Alaska would cost, but they did know they did not even have enough money for their fares across the United States! Sharing this fact with no one, but trusting God to meet their needs, they left Rochester by train for Buffalo at 2:28 in the afternoon on Friday, September 7, 1917. John Wright Follette, Jacob Mueller, Fred Drake, Wilbur Mead, Ethel Walton, and Clara and Lydia Enslin went to the station to see them off. As the train pulled out, they all sang, "God Will Take Care of You."

At Buffalo the Personeuses boarded the steamer *City of Cleveland* and crossed Lake Erie to Detroit. There they visited friends and spoke about Alaska in the Sunday services. According to their journal, they received an offering of $7.00.

From Detroit the Personeuses traveled by train to St. Louis, where the three-year-old Assemblies of God had its headquarters in 1917. The General Council was in session in St. Louis, and the Personeuses were given 10 minutes in the missionary service Sunday evening to speak about their Call to Alaska.

Stanley H. Frodsham, who was serving as the General Secretary and Missionary Treasurer of the Assemblies of God, urged the Personeuses to join the Assemblies of God before going to Alaska, so they arranged to meet with the leadership. At the meeting with E. N. Bell, J. W. Welch, J. R. Flower, and Stanley Frodsham, they received appointment as the first Assemblies of God missionaries to Alaska, but the brethren were unable to promise any financial support.

After the General Council session closed, the Personeuses remained in St. Louis for the rest of the week, helping to proofread the *Pentecostal Evangel* and speaking in area churches. When the brethren learned that the Personeuses were both printers, they asked them if they would work as printers at the new Headquarters, which was being moved to Springfield, Missouri. The Personeuses declined, explaining that he had obtained his military deferment on the basis that he was going to Alaska as a missionary. The brethren agreed that he should go and do the work he had declared.

From St. Louis the Personeuses took the train to California, passing through high mountains such as they had not seen in the East. In California they visited Florence's younger brother George, their father's namesake, who was attending Torrey Bible Institute near Los Angeles in preparation for missionary service in Ecuador. This visit was the last time Florence saw George, for he died of typhoid spinal meningitis in Ecuador four years later, after being on the mission field only nine months.

The Personeuses spent three weeks in the Los Angeles area, speaking in churches, visiting and sightseeing with George. One afternoon they heard the famed Billy Sunday preach. Another day they visited an ostrich farm, where Florence rode an ostrich. They also witnessed their first forest fire, which they described as a "beautiful but terrible sight."

Saying "goodbye" to George, the Personeuses traveled to Oakland, where they were invited to stay with Carrie Judd Montgomery at her faith home, Home of Peace, the first faith healing home on the West Coast. Their money had run out. And they were told that soon the ports of Alaska would freeze up for the winter, and they would have to wait until spring. In Alaska they learned their informant was as misinformed as they were!

Confronted with this situation, the Personeuses began to do the one thing they knew to do. They spent the day in fasting and prayer. The next day they received a letter from a lady in New York whom they could not even remember. She wrote, "I don't know where you might be, but I'm sending this letter in care of Mrs. Montgomery in the hopes that she will be able to forward it to you."

The letter contained a check. That money proved to be enough to pay their fares to Juneau, Alaska's capital city, with enough left over for them to live on until Christmas, when they received more funds.

The Personeuses continued by train to Seattle, where they boarded the *S. S. City of Seattle* and sailed for Alaska. As the steamer puffed out of Puget Sound and turned toward the Inside Passage of Southeastern Alaska, the Lord gave them this verse: "When he brings out his own sheep, he goes before them" (John 10:4).

Typically, it was raining as they left Seattle, but the weather cleared about noon, revealing the spectacular "Inside Passage," where steep, tree-clad mountains rise abruptly from sheltered fjords to lift their glacier jeweled crowns to the sky. The Personeuses proved to be good sailors, not getting seasick even when the deep, rolling swells of the open ocean caused others to get seasick as they crossed Queen Charlotte Sound.

On November 14, 1917, after a five-day trip from Seattle, their ship sailed up Gastineau Channel and the lights of Juneau, twinkling against the dark mountains, came into view, and the Personeuses landed in Alaska's capital city at 7:00 o'clock in the evening.

That morning as Florence had awakened from sleep, the Scripture reference, Philippians 4:19, kept repeating itself in her mind, but she could not remember what verse it was.

"Carl, what are the words of Philippians 4:19?" she asked. "I awakened with that reference on my mind."

"You know that verse," he replied. "And my God shall supply all your need according to his riches in glory by Christ Jesus."

They realized the Lord was directing them that, as they embarked on their new ministry, they were to trust Him to supply *all* their needs– physical, material, spiritual– and they set out to prove His Word.

CHAPTER 5

FLY IN A SUGAR BOWL

*"But you shall receive power, when the Holy Spirit has come upon you;
and you shall be witnesses to Me...to the end of the earth" (Acts 1:8).*

If you travel approximately half way around the globe from Jerusalem,
where Jesus gave the Great Commission, you will discover the vast land
called Alaska, from the Aleut word meaning "Great Land." In 1917,
Alaska could only be reached by steamer traveling up the "Inside Passage"
from Seattle. The "Inside Passage" is an incredibly beautiful passageway
between the mountains of the mainland on one side and the eleven
hundred mountainous islands of the Alexander Archipelago on the other,
which shelter it from the Pacific Ocean. Rugged mountains luxuriously
clothed in spruce and hemlock drop abruptly into salty fjords. Gleaming
waterfalls cascade over cliffs, and pale blue-green glaciers peek from their
hiding places among towering, snow-capped peaks, some spilling out into
wide rivers of ice that calve into salt water inlets. Some of the islands are
quite large. Along their shores are towns, such as Ketchikan, Wrangell,
Petersburg, and Sitka; Indian villages, such as Metlakatla, Hydaburg,
Hoonah, Kake, Angoon, Tenakee; fox farms; ranches; mining camps; and
fish canneries.

Juneau, the Territory's capital city, is located on the mainland on
Gastineau Channel, a fjord just off the "Inside Passage." Named after Joe
Juneau, who discovered gold there in 1880, the city was primarily a
mining town in 1917, although fishing, one of the main industries of the
Territory, also figured prominently in the economy.

When the Personeuses disembarked at Juneau that cold, rainy
November evening, no familiar faces greeted them. They were strangers
in a strange land. As they walked up the boardwalk street carrying their
heavy suitcases, they heard a church bell. Realizing it was Wednesday,
they wondered if some Christians were gathering for a prayer meeting.
Quickly, they found a room in the Bergman Hotel and set off to find the
church. By then, the rain had turned to snow. They paused at the corner
of Fourth and Franklin and prayed that God would bless their ministry in

Alaska. (Years later, Bethel Assembly of God constructed its first and third buildings on that very corner.)

By the time they found the Methodist church, which was having its prayer meeting, it was so late they were embarrassed to go in.

As they stood outside, an old man ambled up to them, peered into their faces, and asked, "Yare bay new in town, airn't yay?"

A little frightened, they replied, "Yes, we just arrived on the boat."

Looking puzzled, the old man asked, "What deet yay ever come ta theese God-fersaken place fer?"

They responded, "God has not forsaken this place. Perhaps the people have forsaken God."

Just then, an older lady came out of the church, and Mr. Tonning introduced them to Mrs. Hannah Krogh. In the course of their conversation with her, they learned she was a widow, who had come to Juneau with her husband a few years earlier as a Peniel missionary. She had held tent meetings until the snow collapsed her tent.

When the Personeuses told her God had called them to Alaska, she said, "I believe you are an answer to my prayers. I've been praying for someone to come and open a mission for the fishermen, miners, and others who do not go to church. Thousands of men work day and night in the Thane, Treadwell, and Alaska-Juneau gold mines in three shifts. They live in bunkhouses with no families. They need the Gospel."

In St. Louis, God had spoken the name "Klukwan" to the Personeuses. They, however, did not know where it was. Looking it up on a map, they wondered whether God wanted them to go on to Klukwan or remain in Juneau. The next day they contacted Mr. Condit and Mr. Wagner, officials in the Presbyterian Church, who informed them that at that time the Presbyterians had a good missionary in Klukwan. What was needed, they advised the Personeuses, was a mission work in Juneau among the fishermen and miners.

As they visited the other ministers in town, they received the same advice: a mission was needed in downtown Juneau. The Personeuses decided the counsel was from the Lord, so they began to look for a place to start their mission. They did not have much money, but they were able to rent a small storefront on South Franklin Street (then called Front Street). The Finnish landlady also had a small room for rent on Decker Way, a long "street" of stairs up the side of Mt. Roberts. The Personeuses rented both for $15.00.

Mrs. Krogh gave them chairs and an organ that had been in the Peniel mission, which had been closed. She helped the Personeuses to clean and create a place of worship out of that tiny storefront. The first service was held Thanksgiving Day, 1917, and the fifteen people present almost filled the tiny room. The Methodist and the three Presbyterian ministers were among those who attended.

When the Personeuses entered their little room on Decker Way, they felt they had made a mistake in renting it. The room was cold and lacking in modern conveniences. Their small sink had cold water, but they had to share a bathroom with the rest of the occupants. The walls were so thin they could hear every sound from the next room, where two Russian men were living. That winter, Juneau accumulated 20 feet of snow, and the cold Taku winds frequently swept off the Taku Glacier, down Gastineau Channel, and up under the floors of that little apartment perched precariously on the mountainside.

Their first night in their first home in Alaska, as Florence had to almost sit on top of the tiny Yukon stove in order to keep warm, the brooding Carl suddenly groaned, "To think I would bring my wife to a place like this!" He was remembering the luxurious, 27-room mansion in which Florence had been reared.

Bravely, Florence smiled. "Remember how we used to sing at Bible school, 'I'm going through, Jesus, I'm going through'? Now is the time to sing it."

"Can you?" Carl asked incredulously.

She answered by singing the chorus to him, and as he joined in, God's glory came down even in that humble shack. That night God quickened to their hearts His Word: "I will...do better for you than at your beginnings: and you shall know that I am the Lord" (Ezekiel 36:11).

By Christmas, their money was just about gone. The morning before they had landed in Juneau, the Lord had called to their attention Philippians 4:19, "But my God shall supply all your need according to his riches in glory by Christ Jesus." They had come this far by faith, and they resolutely determined to follow the rule, "What we can't pay for we will do without." They had no promise of regular support. When funds began to run low, they began to fast and pray and look for ways to share what they had with others. Down to their last three dollars, the Personeuses shared their simple Christmas dinner with Mr. Tonning, the lonely old man who had befriended them on their first night in Juneau. While they were eating, the *S. S. Jefferson* whistled into port, bringing a bundle of letters containing gifts and offerings of over one hundred dollars. Through the years they often had to spend their last dollar, but they resolutely stayed out of debt. And God always supplied their need, though often just in the nick of time.

Completely surrounded by towering, snow-capped mountains, Juneau clings to the steep lower slopes of Mt. Juneau and Mt. Roberts, with narrow Gastineau Channel lapping at its feet. When the Personeuses first arrived in Juneau, Florence, accustomed to the gently rolling farmland of Lancaster County, felt closed in. "I feel like a fly at the bottom of a sugar bowl," she said. After a number of years in Juneau, they climbed to the top of the 3,819-foot Mt. Roberts. From that lofty vista they could see more mountains and more water on the other side of the islands forming the "Inside Passage." That eagle's perspective helped to relieve her perception of being hemmed in. Later, she was able to pen this poem about the mountains she learned to love.

LOOKING TO GOD

(Read Psalm 121.)

Unto the hills, shall I lift mine eyes
For strength in my time of need,
When the day is filled with trials sore,
And the burdens press hard indeed?

To the mountains tow'ring on every side,
Lifting their heads to the clouds,
Ah, can they help a soul distressed,
Enwrapped in earth's dark shrouds?

Nay, though they rise in strength and might,
With a grandeur all their own,
Can my soul find any help or strength
In masses of earth and stone?

30

'Tis the heathen that pray to such,
To rivers and mountains and sun,
But the Christian finds his help alone
In the Lord, the Mighty One.

Unto the hills shall I lift mine eyes
For help, as through life I trod?
Nay, to the Maker of heaven and earth,
I will look to the Lord my God.

For the Lord is my keeper, day and night,
His eye doth never sleep,
And He can preserve from all evil,
For my Shepherd guards His sheep.

Glorious mountains are round about,
But they only point to God.
'Tis the Lord preserves thy going out,
And thy coming in, safe shod.

Look to the Lord to preserve thy soul,
When the burdens of life press sore,
Keep looking to Him, from this time forth,
Till we rest with Him evermore.

—Florence L. Personeus

When the Personeuses disembarked at Juneau, they found a land where living expenses were extremely high. Food, clothing, fuel, furniture, and building materials all had to be shipped in from the States. Even the salmon that was canned there was first shipped to Seattle, then back to Alaska for sale there. The Personeuses felt very isolated because they had to wait weeks and sometimes months for mail from their loved ones to reach them. In the winter months bitter cold winds drove heat from the poorly built houses. In Southeastern Alaska the ever-present rain and dampness caused floors to rot. Keeping warm was a constant challenge.

People invariably associate Alaska with ice and snow and bitter cold. But Alaska is so vast that were it superimposed on the Continental United States, its northernmost tip would be in Minnesota, and its southern "Panhandle" and the Aleutian Chain would stretch from Florida to Southern California, with as much variation in climate. The land falls naturally into four main climates: The Pacific Coast region, Western Alaska, the Far North, and the Interior. The climate of the Pacific coastal region is the mildest. The Japanese current warms the shores of this rugged, mountainous area, washed by the Pacific Ocean. When this warmer Pacific air collides with the snow capped mountains, heavy rainfall results. The rainy season lasts from January to December, except when it snows!

One newcomer to Alaska, after waiting for more than two weeks for some sunshine, met an old Indian on the street and asked in disgust, "Does it rain here all the time?"

The old Indian slowly and stoically replied, "No, sometime he snow."

When the sun does break through, Southeastern Alaska is incredibly beautiful. But its majestic beauty could not camouflage the filth of drunkenness, immorality, vice, sorrow, misery, and debauchery the Personeuses discovered on the streets of Juneau.

Alaska is known as the Land of the Midnight Sun, yet most of the people walked in the darkness of sin, not knowing Jesus, the Light of the World.

Lofty mountains lift hoary heads to the sky, yet alcoholics, gamblers, and adulterers were chained in the pit of sin and degradation.

Crystal-clear streams splash down steep mountain slopes, yet most of the people had never heard of Calvary's cleansing stream.

Giant evergreens—Sitka spruce, western hemlock, and cedar—luxuriously clothe the mountains, yet the people had not been pointed to Calvary's Tree on which Christ's sacrifice for sin was made.

The Personeuses found a land full of transients. Most came hoping to get rich. A few were searching for adventure—to feel the thrill of landing a 30-pound salmon or a 100-pound halibut, or hunting deer, moose, or mountain goats, or finding a gold nugget. Others came to find work or to see the spectacular scenery. Some were searching for lost relatives; others sought to escape God or their past. Living in tiny cabins or in lonely hotel rooms, these people had no place to call home. Some had found jobs and remained among Alaska's friendly people, who, having been strangers themselves, have sympathy for strangers. Often, however, these people failed to find what they sought. Lonely, depressed, despondent, they sank into sin. Some took their lives; some lost their minds and had to be sent to insane asylums. Men having no place to go spent their evenings in pool halls, saloons, and gambling parlors.

The Personeuses also found many Alaskan Natives needing the Gospel. The term *Native* was used to refer to any of the several Indian tribes of Alaska, as well as the Eskimos and Aleuts. To be called an "Indian" if one were an "Eskimo" and vice versa was very offensive to them, yet to the *Cheechako* (newcomer), the differences were hard to distinguish.

In Southeastern Alaska several Indian tribes made their homes on the coastal islands: the Tlingit, the Haida, and the Tsimshian. The Athabascan Indians inhabited the interior of Alaska, while the Eskimos lived along the Arctic Coast and the Bering Sea. The Aleuts, cousins to the Eskimos, lived on the Aleutian and Pribilof Islands.

The Alaskan Natives, like their cousins, the American Indians, were very susceptible to alcoholism. If they took one drink, they often could not stop. Drunkenness often led to the neglect of their children and homes. One little girl in Juneau was found dead from cold and exposure under her bed where she had crawled to hide from her drunken, fighting parents.

During the winter months spent in Juneau, many Natives would confess conversion. In their summer villages, away from the Christian influence, however, they would backslide into their old superstitions, witchcraft, and drunkenness. For this reason, the many small villages and cannery towns scattered throughout Southeastern Alaska desperately needed Full Gospel churches to help stabilize these new converts during the summer months.

Shortly after their arrival in Alaska, Florence was praying when the Lord gave her a vision of the spiritual condition in Alaska. She saw a mountainside so steep that it required careful climbing to ascend the slope. People were scattered all across its broad expanse. Some were endeavoring to keep their footing. But the vast majority were running pell mell down that steep grade, some laughing recklessly, others with terror on their faces. When they saw the dark shadows of an awful abyss at the foot of the mountain, they tried to stop their downward plunge, but the slope was too steep, their momentum too great, and they plummeted screaming into the abyss. As others rushed on, some would snatch at those they passed, pulling them along, struggling, reaching out frantically for help, for anything to check their downward rush.

Florence felt heartsick as she saw those souls rushing toward destruction with no one to help them. Remembering an experience from her childhood, when she and her brother had run a race down a steep hill, and the fear that had gripped her when she found she could not check her downward momentum, she longed to rescue the poor souls caught in that downward rush of sin. She began to cry and ask the Lord what could be done to save them.

While she was praying thus, the Lord showed her a level place being raised up on that steep mountainside. Several people reached it and were able to stop their downward plunge. With relief and joy on their faces, they began to reach out their hands to help others find this place of safety, so they could begin the upward climb again.

Then she saw that underneath this level place, holding it up, was their humble little mission and the faithful workers. Joy surged through her heart, and she thanked God for that little soul-saving station. But as she gazed out over that mountainside stretching away in the distance with its souls rushing to destruction, she cried out, "But, Lord, that is only one little spot of safety! Look at the rest of the mountain! Oh, send forth more laborers to rescue the perishing!"

That vision so gripped her soul that even into her nineties, her prayer for Alaska was that God would send forth more workers into the harvest field of Alaska.

Over the years, Florence penned many poems sharing the need in Alaska, copies of which she enclosed in all her correspondence:

THE NEED IN ALASKA

(To the tune of "Master, the Tempest Is Raging")

There is a need in Alaska,
For many are bound by sin,
Waiting to hear the Full Gospel,
Will you help—these souls to win?
Carest thou not that they perish?
How can you calmly sleep

While perishing souls grope in darkness
Till someone can find the lost sheep?

What have you done for Alaska
And those who are dying there?
Do you pray for their salvation,
Remembering them in your prayer?
Jesus is able to save them,
If they repent and believe.
Let us give them this blessed Full Gospel
That they may this Light receive.

—Florence L. Personeus

REMEMBER ALASKA

(To the tune of "Heavenly Sunlight")

Up in the Northland, there's a fair country,
The land of Alaska, with glaciers so cold,
And beautiful mountains, grand and inspiring,
But souls lost in sin and far from the fold.

Chorus:
Pray for Alaska, send them the Gospel,
Take it to all, the aged and the youth.
What are you doing to win them for Jesus?
Help us to spread the Full Gospel truth.

Many brave hearts work hard for a living,
Seeking for wealth, and searching for gold,
Giving no thought to God and salvation,
How shall they find the Great Shepherd's fold?

There are dear children, needing the Gospel,
Needing a home, and God's love so true,
Groping in sin, and lost without Jesus,
He who has said to feed the lambs too.

Jesus has said, "Go out in the highways,"
Tell them a Savior has died for their sin.
Soon He is coming, for all who are ready,
Hasten, and help to gather them in.

—Florence L. Personeus

PRAY FOR ALASKA

(To the tune of "Speak, My Lord")

Do you know the need up in Alaska,
Where so many souls are lost in sin?
Do you know they need the Gospel?
Will you pray that we these souls may win?

People there are seeking wealth and treasure,
Digging from the mountains yellow gold,
But their souls are wand'ring far from Jesus,
Who will help to bring them to His fold?

Jesus died to save all tribes and nations,
And He says, "Go, preach the Word to all."
Are you praying for Alaska's people?
Pray that on the Savior they will call.

Pray the Lord of harvest to send reapers,
Pray that God shall meet their every need,
Pray that souls may find the blessed Savior,
For Alaska's people, will you plead?

Refrain:
Will you pray, will you pray?
Pray that Jesus they will learn to know?
Will you pray, every day?
Will you answer, "Yes," if He says, "Go"?

—Florence L. Personeus

THE FLAG OF ALASKA

(To the tune of "Alaska's Flag")

Alaska's flag has a message for you,
With its stars of gold on a field of blue;
The blue would speak of a Call so grand,
To preach the Gospel in the far Northland.

The North Star shines like the star that shone
When Christ came from Glory, for sin to atone.
The "Big Dipper" hangs suspended there,
Like souls undecided, in that land so fair.

Jesus has said, "Preach the Word to all;"
Soon He is coming, to give the last call.
When some from all nations under the sun
Shall stand before Him, will you hear, "Well done"?

They that win souls like the stars shall shine,
And share the joy of the Christ divine.
Souls in Alaska are calling for you,
O child of God, what will you do?

—Florence L. Personeus

**Florence LeFevre became Mrs. Charles C. Personeus
in Rochester, NY, on April 5, 1916.**

**Florence Personeus (3rd from left) with her brothers and sisters
at the LeFevre Home in Strasburg, PA.**

**Students and faculty at Rochester Bible Training School,
winter of 1916-17.**

Teachers at Rochester Bible Training School: the Duncan sisters and John Wright Follette.

Carl and Florence working in the printing office at Rochester Bible Training School.

`CHAPTER 6

FIRE!

"Therefore He is also able to save to the uttermost those who come to God through Him, since He ever lives to make intercession for them"
(Hebrews 7:25).

On New Year's Day, 1918, Prohibition went into effect, closing Juneau's saloons and ushering in an era of prosperity for the Territory. With the money previously spent on liquor, people began buying and building better houses. More and better grocery stores opened. Automobiles were shipped to Alaska. Roads were improved and new ones built for the new cars.

The Personeuses soon realized their tiny mission station was too small. One man remarked, "It's so small you're almost on top of the preacher when you get inside the door." Often, strangers would start in, but back out quickly in embarrassment.

With the offerings received in the mail that first Christmas, the Personeuses were able to obtain a larger meeting place. They rented the old Peerless Saloon for $10.00 a month and converted it into a Gospel lighthouse. They bought an old desk and some tables, and fixed up the "Peerless Free Reading Room," where lonely people could come to write letters and read good literature, which friends in the States had provided.

The building containing the old saloon was a small, one-story frame building, built on piling over the beach, so the tide could come in and out under it. The other half of the building was occupied by a dry cleaning business, with only the usual Alaskan cheesecloth and wallpaper "plastering" the rough board partition between. The loud talking, laughing, and profanity often disturbed the services on the other side of the flimsy wall.

One day the fire alarm sounded in the downtown area. A fire in Juneau in those days was often disastrous. The frame houses burned quickly. At that time, the streets were "paved" with wooden planks, so a big fire often burned the streets as well as the houses.

That cold February day, a gasoline explosion in the dry cleaning establishment next door had ignited the blaze. A crowd gathered on the street opposite the little mission to watch. Smoke poured from the building. The business on the one side of that thin cheesecloth and wallpapered partition was burned to a char, while on the mission side little damage was done. On that flimsy wall in the mission hung a motto—ten letters cut from red cardboard and strung on a thread across the wall, "JESUS SAVES."

Many people looking in the window remarked, "It's a wonder this place didn't go too!" Then they would notice the motto—"JESUS SAVES."

A Jewish friend, coming into the mission, exclaimed, "Well, if you folks aren't the luckiest people I ever saw! It's a wonder you weren't burned out!"

Mrs. Personeus pointed to the motto. "Don't you see?" she asked. "Jesus saves!"

Looking at it thoughtfully, he replied, "It sure looks like it!"

And the Personeuses had an opportunity to tell him more about their wonderful Savior.

Yes, Jesus saves! "He is also able to save to the uttermost those who come to God through Him, since He ever lives to make intercession for them" (Hebrews 7:25). And many times the Personeuses proved that verse in Alaska.

One chilly, damp night a young man staggered into the lighted doorway of the little mission. Shocked and dazed, he dropped into the first chair he came to, sitting hunched over with his head in his hands. The first part of the service was over, and Mr. Personeus had just begun his message, telling of Jesus and His mighty power to save, to keep, and to satisfy the longings of one's soul. The man appeared to be drunk, but he did not make a disturbance, so the service continued. The Christians present were all praying earnestly that the young man might find Jesus as his personal Savior.

At the close of the service the Personeuses went to the man and spoke to him about Jesus and His love.

The young man raised his head in surprise. "Am I in a church?" he asked.

His mind had been so full of his own troubles that he had heard nothing. He looked so distressed and dejected that the Christians were filled with sympathy for him. Touched by their concern, he began to tell his story.

Gus had saved thousands of dollars working for years at the Chichagof Mining Camp on one of the islands. Now he was returning to his home in the States. He had planned to buy a home for his folks. But on the boat to Juneau he had lost most of his money in a card game with two polished gentlemen with smooth, white hands.

"If only I had stopped with those first two games," he groaned. "But when I had doubled my stakes, the fever seemed to grip me. When I began to lose heavily, I just wanted to win back what I'd lost. They kept encouraging me, saying my luck was bound to turn soon. And now most of my money is gone!"

As he realized he had been fleeced by a couple of gambling sharks, his bitterness and hatred grew more intense. The desire for revenge gripped him.

"I have some money left," he said. "I'll put up one more stake. Then, if I lose, I'm going to get them—unless they get me first."

Mrs. Krogh, an old timer in Alaska, said kindly, "Don't try it, my boy. Hold on to what money you have left. You can't win your money back. Those men are probably some of the gambling crooks that haunt the boats. You might just lose your life. Your soul is worth more than your money. Seek the Lord, and let Jesus save you."

"I can't! My heart feels as hard as stone. I've got to get my money back. I can't go home without it. Look at my hands. See those calluses?" he asked fiercely, showing them his toil-hardened hands. "I worked hard to get that money. It belongs to me!"

The Christians pleaded with him to "seek first the kingdom of God and his righteousness," but to no avail.

About midnight, Gus said, "There's no use taking any more of your time. I appreciate your kindness and interest, but I've got to get my money back or get revenge."

As he went out the door and down the street, the Personeuses went home with burdened hearts. All night they prayed for Gus.

At dawn, Mr. Personeus said, "I'm going down to the docks to see if I can find that young man."

"All right," Mrs. Personeus answered. "I'll fix breakfast. See if you can get him to come home with you and have breakfast with us."

Down on the docks, Mr. Personeus found Gus pacing back and forth. His face had grown hard and cold. He looked more like forty than his twenty-some years. He started in surprise when Mr. Personeus greeted him.

A look of surprise and wonder came into his face when Mr. Personeus invited him to come home with him for breakfast. *Why should this stranger care about me and my troubles?* he wondered.

He looked at his watch. "Yes, there's time," he said, then added grimly, "I expect to meet those fellows at 10 o'clock for the last game. If they don't get me, I'm leaving on the boat at noon."

The breakfast was very simple. As they bowed their heads in prayer at the table, the Personeuses felt the presence of the Lord. After breakfast they got out their Bibles for morning devotions.

As Gus accepted the Bible handed to him, he said with awe and reverence in his voice, "I've never held a Bible in my hands before. My people are Catholics. We were taught only the priests could understand the Bible. We never even had one in our home."

"Do you believe the Bible?" the Personeuses asked him.

"Oh, yes, it's God's Word," he answered, "but isn't it too hard for common people to understand?"

He was very surprised when they told him that even children could understand a large portion of it. "Of course, some parts are hard to understand, but it's the best Book anyone can read," they assured him.

After reading the Scriptures, they asked him if he would join them in prayer. "You can pray if you want to," he said, "but I won't be a hypocrite. I couldn't pray with this bitter hatred in my heart. It feels like stone."

"But Jesus can take that hardness away if you'll ask Him."

"Oh, no, He can't. You don't know how much I hate those men and want revenge."

"Do you believe the Bible?"

"Yes, it's God's Word," Gus answered slowly.

Then Mr. Personeus took the Bible and turned to Mark 10:27, and read Jesus' answer to the disciples' question, "Who then can be saved?" "But looking at them, Jesus said, 'With men it is impossible, but not with God; for with God all things are possible.'"

"Do you believe that 'with God ALL things are possible'?" Mr. Personeus asked.

"Yes," Gus answered slowly. "It must be so, because Jesus said so. But my heart will be filled with hate and revenge until I get my money back!"

"Let's pray and tell Jesus all about it. He understands," Mr. Personeus said, as he and his wife got down on their knees and began to pray.

Suddenly, a groan that was half a sob broke from Gus' lips. Then he began to cry out for mercy and forgiveness for his sin and hardness of heart. As he prayed, joy and peace crept into his voice. Then with a note of victory, he exclaimed, "Oh, God, I didn't think You could take this hatred out of my heart, but it's gone!"

Then Gus began to pray for the men who had fleeced him. When he arose to his feet, he looked like a different man. He *was* a different man! The hatred, the bitterness, and the hardness were all cleansed away by the blood of Jesus, and he was a new creation in Christ. With the joy of the Lord on his face he looked years younger.

Just before he left on the boat, the Personeuses gave him the Bible, the first he had ever held in his hands, and encouraged him to read it all he could.

With joy on his face, he said, "I never want to touch another deck of cards. My money is gone, but I have found something far better!"

Later, the Personeuses received a letter from Gus' mother, thanking them for what they had done for her boy. "And we're all reading the Bible and learning more from it every day. We are happy in God's salvation," she concluded.

Yes, Jesus saves—even the most hardened of men.

Of course, not all of the men to whom the Personeuses ministered experienced such a dramatic conversion. The officers and crew of a ship that was docked in Juneau visited one of the mission services. Later, tragedy struck. That ship sank, taking with it the lives of all the crew. Who knows but that in their dying moments they accepted Christ as their Savior because of the little mission on South Franklin. At least they had heard the Gospel and how to get right with God. Without that little mission they would not have had that opportunity.

CHAPTER 7

"THAT WASN'T MY CASE!"

"Confess your trespasses to one another, and pray for one another, that you may be healed" (James 5:16).

In February 1918, Mrs. David B. (Louise) Femmer, a Christian lady in Juneau who was to become a lifelong friend of the Personeuses, offered them her two-room basement apartment rent free. It was warm and clean, and they lived there for three years, just across the street from the Governor's Mansion.

Doing the family wash became a severe trial for Florence. She had to scrub the clothes vigorously on a washboard in a concrete tub. Then she had to hang the wet clothes on a line outside the door, often in a cold wind. Severe pain developed in the joints of her shoulder, arm, and hand. They prayed, asking the Lord to heal her, but she still continued to suffer.

When Florence began asking the Lord why He didn't heal her, He spoke to her heart the words of James 5:16: "Confess your trespasses to one another...that you may be healed." As she searched her heart, she remembered the time her mother had been suffering with rheumatism. At the time, Florence had thought her mother was not in as much pain as she let on. Now as she suffered, she remembered her mother. Obeying the Lord, she wrote to her mother, confessing her fault and asking forgiveness. Writing that letter was hard, but when she obeyed, the Lord healed her completely.

By late summer, a baby would be arriving in the Personeus household. Having only fifty dollars saved for the expenses of the birth of their first child, they decided that Florence would have the baby at home instead of going to the hospital. They had found a doctor who agreed to the arrangement.

On August 30, Florence had been cleaning the house. She had washed the curtains and was ironing them when she realized the birth was imminent. The doctor was called, but the baby did not wait for Dr. Sloane. With Mrs. Krogh and Mrs. Femmer in attendance, little Charles

Byron made his appearance, amid prayer and praise. When Dr. Sloane arrived, the 8½ pound baby was crying lustily, and everyone was praising the Lord.

When Mr. Personeus tried to pay the doctor, he refused to take any money, saying, "No, that was not my case!"

Violent storms are detonated in the Gulf of Alaska when cooled continental air, passing over the high mountain ice fields along the Panhandle coast, is suddenly moistened and heated by the warmer Japanese current. The heated air rises, expands, releases more heat in the form of precipitation. The barometer drops. The wind rises to hurricane force.

The last week of September 1918, one such storm, spawned in the Gulf of Alaska, lashed the Panhandle with disastrous results. In Juneau, Gold Creek invaded the city, as torrential rains could no longer be contained within its banks. Losing its foothold on Mt. Roberts, tons of mud slid off, threatening that part of Juneau clinging to its steep side.

But the most infamous of all was the sinking of the *Princess Sophia* on Vanderbilt Reef between Skagway and Juneau in the blinding snowstorm the night of September 26. The big steamer hung on the reef for a day. On board were hundreds of passengers going south for the winter. No larger ships were within call. Small gas boats set out to give aid, but the sea was rough.

The captain told the passengers it would be safer to remain on the *Princess*. "You might lose your lives trying to scramble onto the smaller boats in these rough seas."

The passengers felt comfortable talking or writing in the lounges or resting in their staterooms. No boats were near when killer waves at high tide lifted the *Princess* from the reef and plunged her gurgling beneath the foaming waters of Lynn Canal.

Consternation, horror, and grief swept all along the Pacific Coast as the word clattered over the telegraph wires: "*Princess Sophia* sinks with all on board."

The Personeuses remembered that for days afterwards boatload after boatload brought hundreds of bodies to Juneau. The sinking of the *Princess Sophia* was one of the greatest tragedies in Alaskan waters.

Mrs. Personeus wrote, "What an illustration of this old world, wrecked on the reef of sin! Small Gospel ships hover near to rescue those in danger. But the old devil, the 'god of this world,' says people are better off if they stay with the ship, than to launch out on the mercy of God, confess their sins, and pull for the Heavenly Shore. If the passengers on the *Princess Sophia* had left the ship before it sank, while help was near, they might have been saved. But when the ship went down, thick oil covered the water. Life preservers kept the passengers afloat, but they smothered in the oil. Likewise, to be near this old world when it sinks beneath the waves of judgment will be dangerous indeed."

A traveler stepped into the mission's reading room. While his ship was in port, he was seeing the sights but thought he would rest awhile. As the Personeuses talked with the young man, they learned he was from Philadelphia. When they asked him if he knew the joy of salvation, he replied, "No, I can't say that I do."

The man listened thoughtfully as the Personeuses shared with him the love of Jesus, who had suffered and died on the Cross to redeem the lost, giving His precious blood to pay the price for sin.   .

The young man agreed with them when they explained how dangerous it was to neglect this great salvation. "I'll think about it," he promised, "but I'm not ready yet."

Just then the ship whistled its warning call. As he walked to the door, they gave him several tracts to read on the boat. Thanking them, he headed down the street toward the dock.

To the Personeuses, this young man was just another stranger with whom they had been privileged to share the Gospel. Several years later, however, they received a letter from this young man. He wrote that he had read the tracts and decided to seek the Lord. In San Francisco he had looked up Glad Tidings Mission and there yielded his life to God. After his conversion he had enrolled as a student at the Glad Tidings Bible Institute. Later, he had met and married a fine Christian girl. He wrote that he wanted to come back to Alaska, where he had first been told about salvation, to work for the Lord. The Personeuses wrote back, encouraging him to come since they needed more workers. Mr. and Mrs. Walter Pearson helped in the mission and later worked in the Bethel Beach Children's Home until Mr. Pearson went to be with the Lord.

CHAPTER 8

ONE OF THE "ALL THINGS"

*"And we know that all things work together for good to those who love
God, to those who are the called according to His purpose"
(Romans 8:28).*

The Personeuses learned that no one was holding services for the prisoners in the federal jail in Juneau, so they talked to the United States Marshall and obtained permission to do so. Some of the prisoners were glad to have something to break the monotony of prison life. Others were thrilled to learn that God loved them in spite of their sin and that there was hope for them. The majority, however, did not appreciate their coming. They preferred to spend Sundays playing cards and smoking in the main tank, as the large day room was called. One prisoner rigged up a container of water on a pipe above the spot where the Personeuses stood. As they led the service, he pulled the string, dumping water on them. Undaunted, they continued with the service.

Another man said, "It's bad enough to be in jail without you coming to preach at us."

Mr. Personeus assured him, "We're not preaching *at* you. We just want to share with you the Good News that Jesus loves you and died for you and wants to save you."

He was not convinced. The Personeuses, however, did not allow themselves to become discouraged.

One wintry Sunday morning as they walked to the jail, their arms overflowing with literature and Bibles, Mrs. Personeus slipped on an icy hill and thudded to the frozen ground, injuring her back so badly she could hardly walk. Mr. Personeus lifted her to her feet and prayed for her right then and there.

"I guess you'd better go back home and lie down," he said, when he saw she was still in great pain.

"No," she said, hanging onto his arm. "If you'll help me, I'll go on to the jail. I feel this is a blow from the devil, and if I give in one inch, I may never walk again."

50

Unable to lift either foot from the ground, she dragged one foot after the other. Slowly, they inched their way to the jail. When they began the service, she was in such pain she could hardly sing or speak. Mr. Personeus told the men what had happened. Seeing the pain on her face, some of the hardened prisoners began to soften. They seemed to realize for the first time that the Personeuses were there because they were really concerned about them, and they began to respond.

After the service, Mrs. Personeus dragged herself home. That evening she attended the service at their little mission, still painfully dragging her feet each step of the long walk, resisting the devil as she inched along.

The next day, the Personeuses asked the small group of Christians to come to their home for a day of prayer and fasting for Mrs. Personeus' healing. About three o'clock in the afternoon, the Lord spoke to her heart, saying, "While you praise, I can work."

She told the folks, "We have prayed enough now. Let's praise the Lord."

As they all raised their hands and began to praise the Lord, the Great Physician touched her back, and she could walk perfectly, without pain, from that time on. Looking back, Mrs. Personeus called that experience "one of the 'all things' that work together for good to those who love God, to those who are the called according to His purpose" (Romans 8:28), because through her injury, the prisoners had begun to respond to God.

Years later, she was examined by an orthopedic specialist for another problem. He said, "You have had a severe injury to your spine some time ago. It's a wonder you are not crippled. Nature has done a good piece of work."

She told him, "It wasn't nature. Jesus healed me."

After little Byron was born, the Personeuses began taking him in the baby buggy to the jail services. Many folks were horrified, but the prisoners were delighted. After the services they would come to the bars and smile and talk to the baby. As Byron grew older, the first words he learned to speak were "How do!" He loved to shake hands with everybody and would eagerly stretch out his hand between the bars, and with a cheery "How do! How do!" would shake hands with those men. Many hardened hearts were touched. They might doubt the love and sincerity of the Personeuses, or even God's love, but not the artless smile of that little child.

Years later, the Personeuses received a letter at Christmas from one of the men they had ministered to while he was in prison. He wrote: "I suppose Byron is a big man now, but I shall never forget when he reached his little hand between the iron bars in that Juneau jail and put it so trustingly in mine. That was the beginning of a new life for me. I thank God you pointed me to Jesus, 'the Lamb of God who takes away the sin of the world.' He took my sins away, and I've been able to show others the way of life."

One Sunday morning as the Personeuses entered the main tank, they noticed a nice looking young man pacing back and forth. He looked completely out of place in that jail. When they started the service, he looked surprised, listened awhile, then grabbed his hat and put it on his head. Though he continued to pace, they could tell he was listening intently as they read from Isaiah 1:18: "Come now, and let us reason together, says the Lord, 'Though your sins are like scarlet, they shall be as white as snow; though they are red like crimson, they shall be as wool.'"

Later, the Personeuses learned the man was a Jew who had studied to be a rabbi. During World War I he had been sent overseas. Then he had come to see Alaska and had fallen in with bad company. He and another young man had stolen a boat. They had been arrested and brought back to Juneau for trial.

He had never been in jail before. That first night he had tossed on the hard cot. Unable to sleep, he had begun to repeat the Ten Commandments until he came to "Thou shalt not steal." Unable to say it, he had begun at the beginning again. The second time he had said it. Then he had realized, "Oh, God, I did steal!" Asking God to forgive him, he had determined to tell the judge the truth.

The judge had been so impressed by his straightforward and honest confession, he had said, "I could send you to the penitentiary, but I believe what you did was more a boyish prank than a malicious act. I'm going to let you off with six months and a day in jail."

During those six months, this young man heard the Gospel every Sunday. Each time the Personeuses came, he would put on his hat, since Jews always cover their heads when they worship, he told them later. During his time in jail, the presence of the Lord was often very real in the services. One Sunday nine prisoners accepted the Lord as their Savior, including the Jewish man's pal.

The Personeuses invited the Jewish man and his friend to visit them in their home when they were released from jail. During their visit Mr. Personeus explained how the Old Testament prophecies of the Messiah are fulfilled in Jesus Christ. The young man listened intently but was still not ready to receive Jesus as his Messiah and Savior. He did, however, accept a New Testament and promised to read it.

The next day, the two young men left on the boat for Seattle. Later, the Personeuses received a letter from the Jewish man saying he had accepted Jesus as his Savior and Messiah before he reached Seattle. He wrote, "I thank God He allowed me to be arrested and put in a place where I had to listen to the New Testament. And I'm glad you folks came to the jail."

About a year later another letter came from this young man saying he was now a guard in one of the large penitentiaries in the States. He wrote, "You know I can empathize with the fellows behind bars, because I know what it's like. I've been there. I take my Bible, the one you gave me, and often read with the boys in their cells at night when they are restless. I have had the joy of leading my first convert to the Lord Jesus Christ."

One man the Personeuses met at the federal jail services appeared to be under deep conviction, but he refused to surrender to the Lord. They talked with him many times, but to no avail. When he was to be released, they invited him to visit them in their home. Finally, he came. After supper, they all went to the mission for a service. That night the man told them he wanted to become a Christian, but he was afraid. He knew he would have to confess something that could put him behind bars again. The Personeuses talked and prayed with him until he finally called on the Lord to save him from his sin.

The next day the man went to the judge and confessed his wrong. When he returned, his face was beaming. "Praise God, it's all right! God has forgiven me and so has the judge. He told me, 'I think you are on the right track now. There are no charges against you.' Now I can start my life anew!" He was truly free!

The Personeuses loaned him money so he could go to Wrangell to find employment. Later, he returned the amount he had borrowed, but since he could not write English, they heard no more from him.

53

Thirty years later, the Personeuses were asked to build a church in Pelican. Ground had been donated, but they had no tools for clearing the land.

One day, a man stopped Mr. Personeus on the boardwalk of Pelican. "Well, Mr. Personeus! What are you doing here?"

Not recognizing the man, Mr. Personeus answered, "We're planning to build a church here."

Finally, the man asked, "Don't you remember me?"

"No," Mr. Personeus admitted.

"I'll never forget you and what you did for me when I was down and out." Then the man reminded him of the one they had led to the Lord years before. "If there's anything I can ever do to help you, just let me know."

This man gave them the axes, saws, and other tools they needed for building. "Cast your bread upon the waters, for you will find it after many days" (Ecclesiastes 11:1).

CHAPTER 9

QUARANTINE!

"The Lord will give strength to His people" (Psalm 29:11).

The winter of 1919-20 lives in infamy as the year of the great influenza epidemic. Juneau was hit hard, and many people died. All the schools, churches, theaters, and other public gathering places were closed. Before going outside, everyone had to put on masks.

Just before the quarantine had been put into effect, the Personeuses had met a family that had recently moved to Juneau. The family had not had time to make any friends before the city was quarantined, and no visiting was allowed.

One morning as the Personeuses were having family devotions, Mrs. Personeus felt a great burden for this new family. Leaving the baby with her husband, she walked the five blocks to the family's home. The ominous "Quarantine" card was on their door, forbidding entrance, but she knocked anyway.

The door opened a crack, and the mother cried, "Aren't you afraid of us?"

Quickly, Mrs. Personeus stepped inside and sent the mother back to bed. The entire family was very sick. They were without food. Piles of dirty clothes needed to be washed. Mrs. Personeus got busy on the washboard. Soon the clean clothes were hung out on the line to dry. Then she hurried home and made a big kettle of soup for the family.

Later, when Mrs. Personeus told Dr. Sloane what she had done, he scolded, "Remember, you have a baby and a husband to think of." Then he admitted, "But I wish I had a dozen women like you!"

All that winter the Personeuses, with the permission of the doctor, worked as angels of mercy caring for the sick. And all that winter God protected them from sickness.

Then, when the epidemic was almost over, Mr. Personeus contracted a very bad case of the flu. A wealthy man living near them had had a similar case. Unable to stop hiccupping, the man had been rushed to the hospital. Everything possible had been done to save him, but he died.

Fearing for her husband's life, Mrs. Personeus went to the telephone and called every minister and Christian she knew in town and asked them to pray for Mr. Personeus. God answered their prayers and spared his life.

As a tragic result of that epidemic, many children were left orphaned or with only one parent. These single parents, needing to earn a living, had to find care for their children while they worked.

One father approached the Personeuses. His wife had died, leaving him with three small boys. He had a job, but no one to take care of his children while he worked. "I can take the oldest boy to work with me, if you folks would watch the two younger ones," he pleaded.

The Personeuses agreed, saying, "They can play with our little boy."

Next, a lady visited them. She had heard they were caring for two boys. Her husband had died, and she had four children. "I have a job in a restaurant, but I'm on the night shift. I need someone to care for my children all night," she explained.

The Personeuses were living in the Femmers' two-room apartment, so they had no room for four more children. After prayer, however, the Lord impressed them that they could reach many souls for Him through a children's home. They knew they would need workers if they were to add this responsibility to their work, so they began to pray for two things: workers and a large house.

Meanwhile, in California, God was preparing Mrs. Julia Costigan for this ministry. For 53 years she had lived in New York City, a wealthy member of a fashionable Episcopal church, knowing nothing of the new birth experience that changes lives and satisfies the soul. Now widowed, she and a Unitarian friend were looking for an apartment in California.

The day was warm, and after looking at several apartments, they were tired. Looking for a place to rest, they spotted a large tent.

"Let's go in," Mrs. Costigan suggested. "Perhaps it's a circus. At least we will be able to sit down and rest awhile."

When they got inside, however, they discovered it was not a circus but a Pentecostal meeting! People were testifying and praising the Lord.

The two women had never been in a Pentecostal meeting before. When someone shouted, "Hallelujah!" the ladies jumped, and the Unitarian lady laughed. But Mrs. Costigan, fascinated by the sweet, happy faces, said, "Don't laugh. These people are sincere."

When the service was dismissed, the two ladies disappeared into the crowd. They were rested in body and amused at having found a church service rather than a circus in that tent. But Mrs. Costigan could not forget that meeting. She had caught a glimpse of a joy and peace she longed for.

The next day she went to that tent again, but this time she went alone with no one to disturb her. She listened to an old-fashioned Gospel message that told of the great price Jesus had paid to bring us salvation. When the altar call was given, the worldly-wise lady from New York City went forward. All her self-righteousness was swept away as she confessed her need of a Savior. What a joy and peace filled her soul as she realized she was now a child of God!

As she arose from her knees, a lady told her, "Now you want to ask God to fill you with the Holy Spirit."

Looking up eagerly, Mrs. Costigan responded, "Oh, is there more? Then I want it right now."

She knelt again at the altar and in simple, childlike faith, prayed for and received the baptism in the Holy Spirit.

As praises to God burst from her lips, the power of God swept over her frail body and healed her of a heart condition that had threatened her life. Old things *had* passed away. Yes, all things *had* become new in her life.

Then she realized she was no longer her own. She had been bought with a price, the blood of Jesus. Christ was her Master from now on, so she asked Him, "Lord, what will You have me to do? Where do You want me to go?" And the Lord spoke to her heart, "Go to Alaska."

Eagerly, she told the saints around her, "The Lord has told me to go to Alaska."

Looking at her frail body, they replied, "That's impossible! You must be mistaken."

Puzzled that these more mature Christians could not understand her Call, she kept these things to herself, looking to God for guidance.

While waiting for the Lord to open up the way for her to go to Alaska, she studied the Word of God and grew in wisdom, grace, and spiritual knowledge. Then she read in a Pentecostal paper a letter from missionaries in Alaska. At once she began corresponding with them and discovered she was needed in Alaska very much.

People had told her, "You are too old to go to Alaska." "You could not stand the cold." "You could not learn a new language at your age."

"No church will send you up there." "You are not strong enough." "How will you get support?"

Everyone tried to discourage her, but she obeyed God anyway. When she arrived in Alaska, she discovered she did not have to learn a new language. She was not too old to go to Alaska. She found she could stand the cold. She was needed very much to work among the children in Juneau, and the Lord increased her strength and supplied her needs. She lived to the ripe old age of 89.

With one prayer answered by the arrival of Mrs. Costigan, the Personeuses and she began looking for a suitable house. They found one they thought would be satisfactory, and the rent had been reduced from $35.00 a month to $22.50. They decided to wait until after dinner to rent the house. When they approached the landlord, he told them he had just rented the house 20 minutes before.

Disappointed, they returned home and fell on their knees in earnest prayer. As they prayed, the Lord spoke to Mrs. Personeus, "Get up off your knees, and I will show you the house I have for you."

Praising the Lord, she and Mrs. Costigan set out to look for the house. As they walked, the Lord would impress them to go right or left until they discovered a "For Rent" sign. The house seemed too small for their needs, but they received no further leading from the Lord.

By this time Mrs. Costigan was tired, so she headed back home, but Mrs. Personeus continued on. She had not gone far when she met the Presbyterian minister.

"Have you found a house yet for your children's home?"

"No," she replied.

"Have you asked Mr. Shattuck?" he asked.

So Mrs. Personeus went to Mr. Shattuck's house to inquire if he had any houses for rent. "Yes, I have three houses for rent. Two of them have five rooms and one has nine."

"May I look at the nine-room one?" she asked.

As they walked back past the house she had seen with the "For Rent" sign, she learned it was one of the five-room houses. Further down the block was the large nine-room house that had belonged to Judge Delaney. Inside, she observed a good carpet on the floor, a large china closet, a large table, and the kitchen contained a large range. The house had many nice features, far better than anything else she had seen thus far.

"How much did you say the rent is?" Mrs. Personeus asked.

Mr. Shattuck looked around. "The house is awfully dirty, and it needs repairs, but if you will clean it and do the repair work yourselves, you can rent it for $15.00 a month."

Mrs. Personeus could hardly wait to get home with the good news. Upon further inspection, Mrs. Costigan thought it was too dirty, but Mr. Personeus felt it was the best house available in town, so they rented it. With a lot of soap and water and hard scrubbing, they soon had the place looking spic and span.

There the Personeuses opened the first children's home in Juneau, the Bethel Children's Home. The Presbyterian minister provided bedding and helped to furnish the house. The Delaney house served as a children's home for nine years.

Up to this time the Personeuses had been teaching classes in the Methodist Sunday school, because their mission did not reach many children. Now, with so many children under their care, they began the first Assemblies of God Sunday school in Alaska. Their purpose in operating the children's home was not only to provide the necessities of life to homeless children, but also to give them the affection and attention they so craved. But, above all, they wanted to lead the children to a saving knowledge of Jesus Christ, to teach them how to be happy, victorious Christians, useful in the Kingdom of God and in society.

Some of the parents paid for the care of their children, but others could not. Yet, all the children had to be fed, clothed, and kept warm. The Personeuses still did not receive regular support, and they often had to spend their last dollar to keep the work going. They resolutely stayed out of debt, however. God had promised to supply all their needs, and they continued to follow the rule, "What we can't pay for we will do without." Many times they fasted and prayed. Other times they would look through their meager belongings to see what they could give to others, because Jesus had said, "Give, and it shall be given unto you." And because Jesus had said, "Gather up the fragments that nothing be lost," they learned to be very frugal and careful to never waste anything. And the Lord always met their needs.

To feed their big family, they had to bake 18 loaves of bread twice a week. One morning as Mrs. Personeus prepared to bake bread, she discovered the flour bin was empty.

"My pocketbook is empty," Mr. Personeus replied when she told him, "and the coal is nearly gone too."

They had read how George Mueller, who by faith operated an orphanage in England, had sung the Doxology over an empty flour barrel, so Mr. Personeus asked, "Do you think you could sing the Doxology over the empty bin?"

"I can if you'll help me," she replied.

Gathering all the children around the empty flour bin, they joined hands and sang, "Praise God from whom all blessings flow...." Then they went about their day's work.

About mid-morning, Mrs. Personeus heard a knock at the door. A man she did not know stood there with a 50-pound sack of flour on his shoulder. He carried it into the kitchen, then went out and brought in another large sack.

"But I didn't order these," Mrs. Personeus protested.

"My orders are to deliver them here," he replied, "and they're all paid for."

A little later, a coal dealer delivered a load of coal, filling the bin. Once again Mrs. Personeus explained she had not ordered the coal.

"Well, it's all paid for, and I was told to deliver it here," he said.

The Personeuses never learned whom God had used to supply their needs that day. Perhaps an angel delivered the orders. But once again God had proven Himself faithful. Again they joined hands and sang the Doxology over the bins that were now full, while tears of thanksgiving coursed down their cheeks.

Mrs. Personeus had to do all the wash for all the children on a washboard in the bathtub. One night as she was scrubbing clothes after all the children had been sent to bed, she heard one of the boys talking. Going to the bedroom door to tell him to be quiet and go to sleep, she realized he was praying.

"Dear Lord, bless Mrs. Personeus. She takes such good care of us. Please help her with that big wash."

Deeply touched by his childish concern for her, she crept back to her work, adding a few salty tears to that soapy wash water.

The only doctor the Personeuses relied on completely was Jesus, the Great Physician. He administered healing many times in the Bethel

Children's Home. Mrs. Costigan had a sweet, childlike faith and was a mighty prayer warrior. When a child was injured or sick, she and the Personeuses would pray until the victory came.

When little Byron was not quite three years old, he was playing with several older boys in the home when a heavy plank fell on his knee. It looked as though the bone was crushed, and he could not put any weight on his leg. Immediately, his mother and Mrs. Costigan, whom he called "Codadee" because he could not pronounce "Costigan," began to pray for him. Little Byron prayed too. Following prayer, "Codadee" took one hand and his mother took the other hand, as they all thanked and praised Jesus for healing him. Then, slowly they began to walk, praising Jesus for the victory. Jesus touched that knee, and soon he was walking and putting weight on both legs.

In the Bethel Children's Home were children of many nationalities, from the fairest blonde Scandinavians to the dark-skinned Natives and Filipinos. The Personeuses and "Codadee" loved them all, just as Jesus does. Some of the white parents, however, objected to having their children in the same house with the Native children. Because of this strong prejudice at that time, it seemed advisable to start another home especially for Native children.

Miss Christine Peterson, who had come to Juneau in 1922, and Mrs. Hannah Krogh found a large house a mile outside of Juneau on the beach of Gastineau Channel, had it remodeled, and opened the Bethel Beach Children's Home. Many half-native children, especially little girls, found shelter there. These beautiful children were often deserted by their white fathers and neglected by alcoholic Native mothers. At the Home they found the love and care they so desperately needed. It was in this children's home that the Walter Pearsons worked when they returned to Alaska.

About ten years later, Mr. and Mrs. Wilbur Arketa opened another children's home for neglected Native children. One boy they rescued from drunken parents and raised as their own son later wrote the Personeuses: "How I wish I were through Bible school and ready to go into the Lord's work. Of course, I work for the Lord now, doing what I can. But if the Lord tarries, I hope to do more when I get to be a man, and that won't be long, for I'll be 15 next month. I feel that I'm called to do the same work Mom and Dad [Arketa] are doing. I can remember when they picked me up out of a dirty hut and gave me a Christian home. They not only saved my life, but they were the means of my soul being saved, so I have hopes of doing the same for my people some day. I have been seeking the baptism in the Holy Spirit, and have never had such a happy experience as when I'm under the power. Pray for me that I will soon receive. Raymond Paul Arketa."

CHAPTER 10

"IT DON'T RUB OFF!"

"Pure and undefiled religion before God and the Father is this: to visit orphans and widows in their trouble…" (James 1:27).

After the service in the corridor of the jail one Sunday, one of the men in the tank came over to the bars to talk to the Personeuses. "My wife is a stranger in the city," he said. "She came to Juneau with me for the trial, hoping I would be acquitted. But now I'm in jail, and I don't know how my wife and children are doing. Will you visit them?"

Mrs. Personeus promised she would, so the next day she looked them up. She found them living in a small apartment in a cheap rooming house. As she entered the apartment, she saw the mother lying on a bed in the corner. A little boy about eight years old had opened the door when she had knocked, and two younger boys sat on the floor amid a pile of dirty clothes. A baby girl whimpered beside her sick mother, who was also crying. Little Henry, the oldest boy, was trying to take care of the younger children as well as his sick mother in that dirty, dreary two-room apartment.

As Mrs. Personeus talked with the mother, she cried, "Just look at my keeds. They are all dirty. Their clothes are all dirty, and I'm so seeck I can't wash them. What can I do? I have no money, no friends, no food, and I'm too seeck to work or do anything."

Mrs. Personeus patted her shoulder. "Don't worry. Jesus loves you, and He sent me here to help you. I'll come over tomorrow and wash the clothes for you. God says, 'Call upon Me in the day of trouble; I will deliver you, and you shall glorify me'" (Psalm 50:15).

At that, the woman seemed to brighten a little, seeing a flicker of hope.

After bathing Susie's face and combing her hair, Mrs. Personeus prayed for her, asking the Great Physician to touch and heal her.

"I'm going to go home and make you a big kettle of hot soup now," Mrs. Personeus promised as she left.

On her way home, she stopped at the office of the Alaska Native Service to report the needs of this destitute family and arrange for financial assistance. Later, Mrs. Personeus returned to the tiny apartment carrying the kettle of soup for the family's supper.

Returning the next day with laundry soap, Mrs. Personeus began a washday she would long remember. There was no washing machine, only an old tub and a washboard. A five-gallon oilcan, which had been split lengthwise and placed on its side on the stove, served as a water heater. What a bunch of dirty clothes! She washed and rubbed and scrubbed and rinsed one pile after another, then hung them out on the line to dry.

It was a sunny April day, the Personeuses' fourth wedding anniversary. Mrs. Personeus was glad she could leave the door open as she tackled that pile of dirty, smelly clothes. Henry helped all he could, but Susie, still weak from the fever and malnutrition, had a badly swollen jaw from an abscessed tooth. She lay on the bed in the other room, keeping baby Juanita off the floor. The other two boys, George and Davy, played or looked out the window.

As Mrs. Personeus washed clothes and hung them out on the line on the front porch, a couple Native children next door watched the white missionary intently. When she went back into the house and was scrubbing away on the washboard, they peeked in the door, and then began to sneak quietly toward her. But when she turned her head to look at them, they ran for the door with such wild, frightened looks on their faces that she was puzzled.

She asked Henry, "Who are those children?"

"Oh, that's Peter and Jessie. They come from Yakutat, a village on the Gulf. Their uncle got killed, and their folks has to go to court and tell about it. That's why they came here. The law brought them. They never went to school yet, and they never saw white folks before. They don't know English."

Again Mrs. Personeus bent over her washing. Again she heard stealthy footsteps behind her. Again when she turned her head to look at them, they ran for the door. Again she turned back to her washing. When she heard the footsteps behind her the next time, she determined not to look at them but to wait and see what they were up to.

She felt, rather than heard, their coming—short, excited puffs of breath close to her ear. Then a little brown hand reached out quickly and rubbed her cheek vigorously. The children ran for the door, where they carefully examined the little girl's hand, talking in Tlingit between themselves.

Henry had come from the other room just as Jessie had completed her detective work. He laughed and said, "They never got so close to white folks before. They think you put white stuff on your face. They thought it might rub off."

Happily, Henry helped Mrs. Personeus gather in the dry clothes to make room for more clothes on the line. The pile of clean clothes was growing. Then he found a mop and began mopping the floor and cleaning up the tiny apartment. As they worked, Mrs. Personeus told him about Jesus and His great love for everybody.

"Would you like to come to Sunday school?" she asked.

"I'd like to if Mom don't need me." Henry looked at his mother with a longing question in his eyes. She smiled and nodded her head that he could go.

The next day the family was able to get food and fuel, and Susie received dental care through the assistance of the Alaska Native Service. They also supplied her with hair seal skins and beads so she could make moccasins to sell. She was growing stronger each day.

On Sunday, Henry was all ready to go to Sunday school when the Personeuses stopped for him. Little George was ready too.

"You can all come," Mrs. Personeus told Susie.

But Susie shook her head. "Davy is too shy, and Juanita is too little. She cuts teeth and cries. I got no shoes yet. Some day I come."

Just then, Peter and Jessie peered curiously in the door.

"Why don't you invite them to come too?" Mrs. Personeus asked Henry.

Henry looked sad and shook his head. "They don't understand what you say. They couldn't learn nothin.'"

Suddenly, he brightened, and turned to them and began to jabber in Tlingit. They looked pleased and excited.

"They want to come," Henry said. "They say they are not afraid of you now. If you tell the Bible story real slow and simple, then I can tell them in our language what you say, so they can learn too."

Pleased at his interest, Mrs. Personeus agreed. "That's fine. You can be our interpreter."

Though Henry was a very young interpreter, he must have made the Gospel clear and plain, for Peter and Jessie learned to love God and gave their hearts to Jesus. So did Henry, George, Susie, and eventually Henry's daddy, Joe. When Joe was released from jail, the family went back to their own village, taking the good news of salvation with them. Those children grew up to follow Jesus. Sadly, little Henry did not live to grow up, for one day he fell off a boat and drowned, but he had done his part in spreading the Gospel.

CHAPTER 11

A MACEDONIAN CALL

"Is anyone among you sick? Let him call for the elders of the church, and let them pray over him, anointing him with oil in the name of the Lord: and the prayer of faith shall save the sick, and the Lord will raise him up..." (James 5:14,15).

One chilly evening in November 1921, the Personeuses' fourth winter in Alaska, a Tlingit Indian man in his late thirties came into a service of the mission in Juneau. After listening intently to the testimonies and the message, he suddenly stood to his feet and in broken English said, "You people can read Bible. My people no read. We want preacher. You come Klukwan. Teach Bible. You come?"

As he sat down, a stunned silence filled the room. The Personeuses had recognized *Klukwan* as the name the Lord had spoken to them several years earlier, even before they had come to Alaska.

Mrs. Hannah Krogh stood and said, "I feel this is like Paul's 'Macedonian Call.'" Turning to Mr. Personeus, she continued, "If you feel you should go, I will take care of your work here at the mission until you come back."

Then Mrs. Julia Costigan, the Personeuses' assistant in the Bethel Children's Home, rose and said, "And I will take care of the children's home."

Feeling God had set His seal of approval on the Call, the Personeuses began to prepare for the trip to Klukwan, the winter home of some Tlingit Indians, located about 85 miles north of Juneau. (During the summers the Indians worked in the salmon canneries or fished among the coastal islands, stocking their caches for the winter with salted and smoked fish.) The Personeuses learned that Klukwan had a small frame church with a parsonage attached that belonged to the Presbyterians, but the pulpit had been empty since World War I. Mr. Personeus obtained permission to use the old church and parsonage.

Early New Year's Day, 1922, at the close of the watch night service at the mission, the Personeuses said "good bye" to their co-workers and set out for Klukwan. The first half of the trip was to be made by mail boat up Lynn Canal, the northernmost portion of the Inside Passage, to Haines. As they prepared to board, they learned that the mail boat had been blown upon the rocks in a storm and was being repaired, so a smaller boat was taking the mail north.

Looking at Mrs. Personeus, the captain apologized, "It's no boat for a lady!"

But they were all packed and ready to go, so they went on board. "There's a small cabin at the stern if you want it," the captain offered.

Fat snowflakes were beginning to fall, so they headed for the cabin. There they found several inches of water sloshing about on the floor. The two bunks were filthy. They were unable to latch the door, so the cold wind blew snow in their faces as they sat on the bunk, but that is probably what saved their lives that night. They were thankful for the old fur coat Mrs. Krogh had given Mrs. Personeus, and the fur cap for Mr. Personeus, as well as the heavy, warm overcoat for little Byron.

The boat left Juneau at one o'clock in the morning, heading for Haines, about 80 miles north. Lynn Canal can be glassy calm at times, but it was dark and stormy as the bow of the small craft cut the waves whipped up by the blizzard. After several hours, Mr. Personeus went out on deck to get some fresh air. When he returned, he realized the tiny cabin was full of gas fumes from the exhaust pipe just outside the swinging doors. His wife and son had become quite drowsy and were just dropping off to sleep, so he quickly dragged them out on deck and up to the forecastle near the bow, where they stayed for the rest of the trip. When they finally reached Haines, their trip to Klukwan had to be delayed for 10 days while they recuperated from the effects of the carbon monoxide poisoning that had made them deathly ill.

The second lap of their journey was made by horse drawn sled over an icy trail along the Chilkat River. It was January 13, Mr. Personeus' thirty-fourth birthday. Early that morning, two Tlingit men helped Mr. Personeus load their baggage, bedding, Byron's crib, a trunk, and food supplies for the rest of the winter on the flat sled. Then they started out for Klukwan, accompanied by the two Indian men.

They had only gone six miles when they rounded a sharp bend and found the trail had been swept clean of all snow by the strong wind, leaving only icy ruts. The load on the sled was too heavy to be dragged on the rough, frozen ground.

"Get out sled. Walk," ordered the owner of the team.

Mr. Personeus helped the two Indian men unload half the baggage beside the six-milepost, then went with the men to help push the sled over the rutted, frozen ground, leaving Mrs. Personeus and Byron to follow on foot—alone.

That four-mile stretch was lonely, and the going was hard. The howling of wolves in the distance broke the silence, sending shivers of fear down their spines. When little Byron stumbled on a rut, his mother would pull him up by the arm until he complained, "Mama, you're pulling my arm off!" Then she lifted him up by the collar of his tightly buttoned overcoat.

On they stumbled, exhausted and numb with cold. Finally, they reached the Indian cabin at the 10-milepost, where they were to wait for the sled. As they approached the tiny, one-room log cabin, Tom Canuk's sled dogs ran snarling and howling toward them. Hot fingers of fear clutched their hearts, for Alaskan sled dogs, part wolf, were capable of tearing a human being apart in minutes! Aroused by the ruckus, the owner called them off just in time.

Safe at last in the cabin, they were able to rest on blocks of wood that served as chairs and eat a cold lunch, while mice chased each other on the dirt floor. They were only half way to Klukwan. The entire trip usually took six hours, but they had already used up most of the daylight of that short winter day.

When the sled and the men arrived with the second half of the load, they reloaded and continued on to Klukwan. At 13-Mile they had to again unload the baggage because the horses were giving out. It was dark, so they had to leave the remaining baggage by the side of the trail to be brought in the next day. When the Personeuses arrived in Klukwan at 10:30 that night, it had taken 13 hours to go 23 miles.

When Mrs. Personeus saw Klukwan in daylight, she realized it was the village scene the Lord had shown her in a vision while she was in Bible school. The church consisted of one large, bare room with a pump organ, a pulpit, and chairs for the people. The adjoining parsonage was a frame building also. The first floor consisted of a living room, a kitchen, and a woodshed, where the wood was cut up and stacked for use in the kitchen stove and living room heater. A stairway led up to the bedrooms. The Personeuses kept the door open to the bedroom they used so heat could enter from downstairs. The other bedrooms were freezing cold. In them they kept their perishables. The big bag of potatoes they had brought with them stayed frozen solid all winter. To prepare them for eating, Mrs. Personeus boiled them from the frozen state to keep them from turning black.

Mr. Personeus often had to climb some nearby mountain to cut wood for their heat. One time as he was dragging a log down a gulch, it struck an icy spot and slid down the hill too fast, throwing him off his feet. He was also carrying a long large-toothed saw. When he fell, the teeth of the saw were driven into his knee. He had to be carried home because the pain was so great. One of the Natives told Mrs. Personeus of a man in the village who had been hurt in the same manner and was always lame thereafter. The Personeuses prayed, however, and God healed that knee so that no lameness remained.

Only a few of the Indians spoke English, so the Personeuses had to use an interpreter, who could only speak broken English himself. To make sure the man understood the concepts being taught, Mr. Personeus would spend hours with his interpreter every Saturday, going over the sermon he would preach the next day.

Tlingit is a guttural language, very hard to pronounce or spell, and it had not been written. The vocabulary was very limited, consisting primarily of nouns and verbs. Many common English words did not exist in the Tlingit language. For example, they had no words for *sheep* or *shepherd*. The only animals resembling sheep they had ever seen were the wild mountain goats that live high among the rugged mountain peaks. The Indians hunted these goats and killed them for food. They could not understand the Twenty-third Psalm, which describes a shepherd's care for his sheep. And in Southeastern Alaska the only still waters are along the beaches of the bays and inlets. The fresh water streams are dashing mountain creeks. Thus, one interpreter's version of the Twenty-third Psalm came out like this: "The Lord is my goat hunter. I don't want Him. He knocks me down on the mountaintop and drags me down to the beach." He had missed the point entirely!

Many of the familiar Bible stories were difficult to explain in Tlingit. The temptation of Adam and Eve by "that old serpent, the devil" was one such story, because Alaska has no snakes. The Natives had never seen ants, locusts, or honeybees, and it was hard to explain what they were like. Because grains such as corn and wheat, fruit trees, and grapevines require such a long growing season and a mild climate, they do not grow in Alaska. Neither did the Natives plant gardens; so much of the imagery of Jesus' parables was lost on them.

As these Scriptures were explained further, the interpreter's face would light up with joy as he cried, "I see! I see!" Then the joy would fade. Sadly, he would tell Mr. Personeus, "But I no tell my people. We have no words in our language to tell them. I'm educated. I see, but no tell."

But the Personeuses *were* able to tell these people about the love of the great God who created them and of His only Son Jesus who came to this earth to die for the sins of the world. Many of the Natives grasped the message of salvation and were born again by the Spirit of God. One young man became an earnest worker for the Lord. He got a Bible and learned how to read it. After the Personeuses left Klukwan, he taught it to his people and won many souls to Jesus.

Few of the people in Klukwan had clocks or watches, so they depended on "Elder" Charlie Kladoo, who had a watch, to ring the church bell, which hung suspended on a tripod tower in front of the church, a half hour before services. Then everyone in the village who could walk would come to church. At night, they carried lanterns and long, heavy sticks to keep their half starved sled dogs from attacking them. As they walked, they would swing the clubs, yelling, "Chook! Chook!" The lanterns provided light for the services since there was no electricity.

The Indians loved having church and a preacher. They sang many hymns in their own language. "At the Cross" was a great favorite. Sometimes they brought big blocks of wood for the church heater as an offering. Getting enough wood to keep things from freezing in the houses was a problem when the temperatures dropped to 20 degrees below zero.

Food was also scarce. This was the reason the sled dogs every family kept for hauling wood were allowed to roam loose, so they could forage for food for themselves. The Indians gave the dogs additional food only when they were needed for hauling. The Indians' diet consisted mainly of dried, salted, or smoked salmon, and occasionally, rabbit, ptarmigan, mountain goat, and venison. In the summer wild berries supplemented this diet. They also ate bread if they could buy flour to make it themselves.

Since Klukwan was a winter village, when the weather warmed up in the spring and the river ice melted so they could use their boats, the Natives went down the Chilkat River to Haines to go fishing or work in the salmon cannery for the summer months. Most of the Indians had a cabin in Klukwan and another one in or near Haines, so Klukwan was almost deserted all summer long. The Personeuses were then free to return to Juneau to their mission work and children's home. They also held services in Haines and at the cannery for the Klukwan people.

At the close of the fishing season in September, the people moved back to Klukwan for the winter, asking the Personeuses to do the same. That second winter the school teacher was a bachelor, so Mrs. Personeus was the only white woman in the village. She loved the Indian women and they loved her, but because of the language barrier, conversation with them was very difficult.

Fire is the scourge of the North. People often overheated their stoves trying to keep warm. Whenever a fire broke out in the village, someone would ring the church bell. Then everybody would grab a bucket or a ladder and run to help fight the fire.

One freezing night the fire bell rang. In his hurry to get to the fire, Mr. Personeus forgot one cardinal rule of the North—never run when the temperature is below zero. The icy air froze his lungs, and he returned home coughing and gasping for breath. By the next day, pneumonia had set in, and he was burning up with fever. Klukwan had no doctor, so Mrs. Personeus nursed him the best she could. But he only got worse. She and little Byron prayed for him fervently, but as Saturday dawned, Mrs. Personeus was afraid he was dying.

Finally, Mr. Personeus whispered, "Ask 'Elders' Charlie Kladoo and George Willard to come and pray for me according to James 5:14, 15."

Quickly, Mrs. Personeus donned her coat and went to get them. When she returned with the "elders," she read James 5:14 and 15 to them, explaining what it meant. Giving the bottle of oil to Charlie, she led the way to Mr. Personeus' bed. Standing around the sickbed, the men anointed their preacher with a drop of oil on his forehead and prayed for him. Mrs. Personeus and young Byron joined with them in prayer and praising.

The next morning, the people heard the church bell ring. How happy and surprised they were to find Mr. Personeus well and ready to preach. Mr. Kladoo had told them how sick the preacher was, but there he stood, not looking the least bit like a dying man. Mr. Kladoo gave a wonderful testimony of how they had prayed, and God had healed their preacher. That miracle was a great object lesson on divine healing for the whole village. After that, the sick came to church to be prayed for to receive healing, for there was no doctor for many miles around.

One evening at the close of the service, Mr. Personeus asked if anyone wanted special prayer. A woman who seldom came to church stood and walked painfully to the front of the church for prayer. Mrs. Personeus and another Christian lady, Mrs. Alice Lee, knelt in prayer at the front bench, as Mr. Personeus began to pray for the sick woman. Mrs. Personeus noticed that her husband had begun to pray in tongues, but she was startled when Mrs. Lee suddenly grabbed her arm and whispered excitedly, "He's talking our language!" And they both knew Mr. Personeus could not speak Tlingit.

Mrs. Personeus listened intently. Sure enough, he sounded just like an Indian speaking Tlingit. "What's he saying?" she asked Mrs. Lee.

Mrs. Lee listened carefully, her face becoming very serious as she told Mrs. Personeus the interpretation. "He's saying, 'God loves you. God can heal you. God wants to heal you, but you are hiding sin in your life. God knows your sin. He cannot bless sin. You must tell God you are ashamed of your sin. Ask Him to forgive you and live right. Then God will heal you.'"

The sick woman began to cry. She confessed her sin of adultery, which was known to all the villagers except the Personeuses. Then, as the preacher prayed for her again, she was healed.

The Holy Spirit had used Mr. Personeus in the gift of tongues (1 Corinthians 12:10) in the woman's own language, which he did not know, to pinpoint sin in her life that was blocking her from receiving God's blessings. God also used this incident to show the Indians that although the preacher may not know what they were doing, they could not hide their sin from God. As a result, great reverence for God filled the hearts of the Natives.

CHAPTER 12

"COME IN OUT OF THE MOSQUITOES!"

"To comfort those who mourn in Zion, to give them beauty for ashes, the oil of joy for mourning, the garment of praise for the spirit of heaviness..." (Isaiah 61:3).

Since Klukwan became a ghost town each summer, the Personeuses held services in Haines and Skagway on their way back to Juneau to check on the work there. In Haines they were invited to hold services in a log cabin on a homestead near town. Haines is home of the first permanent Army post in Alaska. Quite a few soldiers stationed at Chilkoot Barracks attended these services. Among them was a good-looking fellow with a fiery temper, named Bill. He brought with him a lady friend, who was unhappily married to a wealthy man. She planned to divorce her husband and marry Bill.

When this lady heard the Gospel, she gave her life to Christ and wanted to be baptized in water. The day before the baptismal service, the lady told Mrs. Personeus of her plans to divorce her husband and marry Bill. After talking with Mrs. Personeus, who showed her God's Word concerning marriage, she decided it would be wrong to do as she had planned.

That evening when she told Bill she could not marry him, he was furious. "I'll shoot you and that preacher if you get baptized tomorrow!" he threatened.

Frightened, she ran back to the house where the Personeuses were staying. About one o'clock in the morning they heard Bill's motorcycle. After awhile, he shouted, "The cabin where you hold services is on fire!"

The cabin and its contents were a total loss. The Personeuses lost a folding organ, books, chairs, and other materials inside that cabin. The lady, however, did not let the fire or Bill's threats deter her from being baptized. That Sunday afternoon, Mr. Personeus baptized her and two others, not knowing if a shot might be fired from the bushes at any moment.

Later, Bill surrendered to the claims of Christ and was baptized. Then he told them how he had been hiding in the bushes that day, but something had kept him from carrying out his threat.

From Haines, the Personeuses traveled on to Skagway, the Gateway to the Klondike Gold Rush of '98, and the first incorporated city in Alaska, where they would fill in for the resident workers of the Peniel Mission (an independent holiness group), who were on leave. In 1898, as many as 5,000 men a month, with their horses, mules, and dogs, had stampeded through Skagway to climb the 3,739-foot Chilkoot and White Pass trails to the Yukon goldfields. Although its population had dwindled from 20,000 at its heyday to 500, Skagway did not become a ghost town after the gold rush because of the railway connection built in 1899 to Whitehorse, in the Yukon Territory. Skagway boasted of streetcar tracks and colorful facades on its solidly built downtown structures. Its cemetery had markers to villains and heroes alike, for next to the grave of the outlaw Soapy Smith stands a monument to honor Frank Reid, an officer who gave his life to bring justice to the frontier. During the gold rush, Evangeline Booth, of the Salvation Army, had come to Skagway to preach to the prospectors and miners. Near the center of town stood the box-like storefront that housed the Peniel Mission.

One evening a young Norwegian couple visited the mission. Gustav and Laura Nyseter had left Norway the year before to embark on a journey that would take them to the "farthest ends of the earth." (They would spend more than seven years on Little Diomede Island, within rowing distance of Big Diomede Island, just across the International Date Line in the Bering Strait. Thus, they became the last missionary contact with Siberian Eskimos before being cut off by the Iron Curtain.) Arriving by ship from the south, they planned to continue their journey by rail to Whitehorse, where they would board a sternwheeler to travel north on the Yukon River to western Alaska. The Personeuses gladly welcomed the Nyseters and invited them to take part in the meetings. Gustav preached and had the unique experience of having his somewhat limited English translated into another language.

While the Personeuses were ministering in Skagway, they felt burdened to go on to Whitehorse in the Yukon Territory, so they decided to accompany the Nyesters on the narrow gauge White Pass and Yukon Railroad. This proved to be a big help to the Nyseters, who had many

75

barrels and boxes to carry. They had come prepared with anything they might need in that remote location.

When the Personeuses arrived in Whitehorse, they found that hotel rooms were very expensive. But God touched the heart of a businessman to give them the use of his small house for a week.

The first morning there, they were surprised to find frost on the ground in June, and the temperature a chilly 28 degrees. By noon, however, the thermometer had soared to over 100 degrees!

The Personeuses witnessed to people they met and held services at the nearby Indian village. But they still felt there was one special person in Whitehorse who needed spiritual help. After spending a day in prayer, they started walking one evening, trusting the Lord to lead them. As they followed one street, they discovered a cemetery.

"Have you ever seen so many graves for little babies?" Mrs. Personeus remarked, as she noticed marker after marker with ages one day to one year engraved on them.

Leaving the cemetery, they walked up another street. The mosquitoes swarming around them were eating them alive in the summer twilight. They were so busy defending themselves against the attack they did not notice two ladies sitting on a screened porch.

"The mosquitoes are bad tonight, are they not?" they heard a lady's voice call out.

Looking up at the house they were passing, the Personeuses agreed.

"Are you strangers in town?" the lady asked.

When the Personeuses said they were, the lady invited, "Come in on the porch away from those mosquitoes."

Feeling this was God's leading, the Personeuses, one at a time, quickly squeezed in the door, brushing off mosquitoes before entering. They found themselves on a wide porch with comfortable, cushioned chairs. Their hostess turned the conversation to names, remarking she had never found anyone with the same name as hers, except one. When she mentioned her name, Mrs. Personeus recognized it as the name she had seen on a white marble shaft in the cemetery. She noted the sad, almost bitter hardness in the lady's lovely, cultured voice.

The Personeuses soon learned the other lady was also a stranger their hostess had called in from the street. After discussing general topics for a while, the Personeuses mentioned how wonderful it was to trust in God.

Bitterly, harshly, their hostess snapped, "Don't talk to me about God. Once I believed in God and thought He loved and cared for people, but not anymore. Oh, no!"

"God does love and care for you," the Personeuses assured her. "Sometimes things happen we can't understand, and it seems to us He doesn't care, but God loves us and can bring blessing out of every sorrow if we let Him."

As the Personeuses arose to leave, their hostess caught Mrs. Personeus by the hand. "Will you come over tomorrow? I want to talk with you some more."

Assuring the lady she would come, they said, "Good night." Now they knew why the Lord had led them to Whitehorse.

The next morning Mrs. Personeus returned to the pretty log house. Warmly, the lady welcomed her and showed her around her home. Then, sitting down, she told her heartbreaking story.

Her voice hard, she told how she had lost her parents while still a child, how she had struggled to get an education, how lonely she had been teaching school in Massachusetts. Then one day she had fallen in love, and her future brightened. But when spring came, he had to return to his summer job as a pilot on a steamer on the Yukon River.

His letters were cheerful and encouraging. Finally, the time came for her to join him, and she began the long journey alone across the continent and up to Skagway. She described her joy when he met her steamer. Her voice softened as she relived in her memory the quiet little wedding in the log church, and the trip on the river with her pilot husband.

How happy they had been together in the little log cabin he had built for his bride. Soon they were eagerly expecting a little one. But after three brief days, their baby had died, leaving greater loneliness and grief.

Her husband had to be away three weeks at a time piloting the boat down the river and back. Her sorrow and loneliness seemed more than she could bear, as day after day she gazed out the window toward the cemetery where their baby was buried, wondering, "Why, oh, why did God take my baby?"

Each time her husband returned, he saw that grief was sapping her vitality. Finally, he suggested, "Why don't you pack up our things and go to Vancouver. Find us a cozy house or apartment. Then when the river freezes up in the fall, I'll come down, and we'll spend the winter together there."

Soon she was on her way south. She found a nice place to live and began preparing for winter. She canned fruit, made jelly, preserves, and pickles—everything her husband liked.

How delighted she had been when the telegram arrived: "Leaving Skagway tonight on *Princess Sophia*."

Only 4 more days! she thought.

Then came the crushing news: "*Princess Sophia* sinks with all on board." She felt she had nothing to live for. Consciousness meant only grief and agony. Her faith ebbed away, as she cried, "Why, oh, why?"

For a year she hung between life and death, but slowly she grew stronger until finally she returned to their little log cabin in Whitehorse.

"But the loneliness is terrible," she sobbed. "Now do you understand why I can't believe there is a God who loves and cares? No, there's nothing but bitter fate."

With a heart full of sympathy and eyes full of tears, Mrs. Personeus softly began to repeat the words of a hymn:

> Oh, yes, He cares; I know He cares;
> His heart is touched with my grief.
> When the days are weary, the long nights dreary,
> I know my Savior cares.

"We cannot understand why these things happen, but don't doubt His love," Mrs. Personeus continued. "Perhaps you were too preoccupied with these earthly loves and failed to give Christ first place in your heart. He suffered the greatest agony anyone has ever known, and He deserves our deepest love. God looks at our lives in the light of eternity. He has something far better for you. Jesus can fill the void in your life and give you greater joy than you've ever known."

Putting her arm around the weeping lady, Mrs. Personeus said, "You say your life has been nothing but disappointments. I've had disappointments and sorrow in my life too. I've learned to spell my disappointments with an "H," and see them as 'His appointments,' and remember that behind each one is a love greater than we can fathom.

"One day when my heart was crushed with disappointment, God gave me this little poem. I wrote it down. Later, these verses helped me through an even greater disappointment."

And Mrs. Personeus began to recite her poem:

78

DISAPPOINTMENT

How oft, as on life's way we tread,
With hopes for future bright,
A cloud comes sweeping o'er our way,
Hiding awhile the light.

These shadows dark that cross our path,
Bringing us grief and pain,
These disappointments, one and all,
God sends for our true gain.

How hard to learn this lesson great;
We know not what is best.
How hard to trust His loving care,
When we feel sore oppressed.

But, if we truly love our God,
Rememb'ring, as we should,
To them, 'twas said, that ALL things
Work together for good.

Ah, then, let each disappointment,
Though great, or only small,
Ever draw us closer to Him
Who loves and cares for all.

Then, if life be full of shadows,
And our path be dark with dread,
Let us look beyond the storm clouds,
To the Light that shines o'erhead.

—Florence L. Personeus

As Mrs. Personeus finished the poem, the lady bowed her head and wept. The hardness and bitterness melted from her face and voice, as she asked, "Will you please write out that poem for me?"

When the poem had been written out, the two knelt in prayer, and Jesus brought His healing balm to the lady's broken heart. Her faith in God was restored and deepened.

A year or so later, she wrote from California saying, "The Lord has filled every aching void in my heart and given me greater joy than I have ever known. I'm happy in His love and service."

CHAPTER 13

THIN ICE!

"Now when the multitude saw it, they marveled and glorified God..."
(Matthew 9:8).

One of the most difficult times of testing the Personeuses experienced began in Klukwan in January 1923, their second winter there. Mrs. Personeus was carrying a bowl of hot food to the home of a sick woman. Walking down an icy hill, she suddenly slipped and both feet flew out from under her. Not wanting to spill the food, she failed to break her fall. When she tried to get up, searing pain shot through her pelvic region, and she fell back in agony. Little Byron, looking out the window, saw his mother sprawled in the snow and called his father, who carried her back to their house.

Mr. Personeus laid her on the couch and prayed for her. The pain eased some, but whenever she tried to get up, she fell to the floor in agony. The only way to get to a doctor was by horse-drawn sleigh or by dog sled, and she was in too much pain to consider either. They kept on praying for healing, but it was at least a month before she was able to walk, though with great pain and difficulty. And there was the added complication that she was expecting their second child in May.

Mrs. Personeus wrote to friends, asking them to pray for her. To her sister in Pennsylvania she wrote, "Unless God undertakes, I don't feel I will get out of Klukwan alive."

Her sister Mary wrote back: "I've been praying for you, and I feel you should come home. You have been in Alaska for over five years now. Come and stay with me, and I will take care of you when the baby comes. I'm sending a check to help pay your fare home."

As the Personeuses thought of the many miles that separated them from their loved ones in Pennsylvania, they felt it was impossible to go. They had not even considered leaving Alaska, but then they received five more letters from different people saying they had been praying for them and felt they should take a furlough.

"But we don't want to leave Alaska," Mr. Personeus said. "Our work here is not finished."

"Maybe it's God's will," Mrs. Personeus replied. "Seven is God's number of completeness. Let's see if we get another letter. If we do, let's take it as a confirmation of the Lord's will for us to go on furlough."

In the next mail was a letter from the Assemblies of God Headquarters with a check enclosed for their fares to Pennsylvania.

By this time it was March, and the baby was due in May. When they asked the Natives if it would be easier to get to the coast in March or April, they were told, "You go March or you no go until May. Ice breaks up in river. Can't go in April. You go dog team now, but not April."

This news startled them. They had been hoping to go to the coast by car on the narrow, winding dirt road that followed the river. But the road was impassable in March. The mountains rose abruptly from the road on one side, and the river lay on the other side. In some places the river was almost even with the road; in other places it was a steep 50-foot or more drop from the road. With no culverts the many streams that ran down the mountainside flowed across the road. All winter the water had been freezing and building up huge mounds of ice across the road, some 10 feet high or more. The Natives called these mounds "glaciers."

When Mrs. Personeus was told they would have to travel by dog sled, she was dismayed. During the winter the Natives made trips to the coast by dog sled for mail or supplies. Sometimes these trips had not turned out too well. One time a man had taken his wife with him to do some shopping, returning with their Yukon sled well filled. Just about a mile from home the dogs had spotted a rabbit and taken off after it, ignoring the sled and the driver. Having no lines with which to hold them back, the driver had yelled at them to stop, but to no avail. The sled dogs, part wolf, were seldom fed by the Natives but were left to forage for themselves. When they saw food, they pursued it. Away they had raced, overturning the sled, dumping the passenger and all her bags and packages along the road, tearing the harness as the sled bounced along behind them, snagging on bushes and trees as the dogs ran. When they had finally torn loose from the sled, they had disappeared. The driver and his wife, shaken up but unhurt, had gathered up their possessions, piled them in the sled, and pushed and pulled the sled home themselves.

Since there was no other way, the Personeuses packed their belongings and prepared for the trip. The Natives selected the two best dog teams in town to take them to the coast. The strongest team would carry their baggage; the fastest team would take Mrs. Personeus and four-year-old Byron. The Lord had told them the date on which to leave, but they waited until after Sunday, and they almost did not get away. An early spring thaw set in, and it began to rain.

One morning, a thunderous roar awakened them. The house quivered. At first, they thought it was an earthquake, but then they discovered a huge avalanche had come down across the road just below the village. It looked as though their route to the coast had been cut off.

It continued to rain, and the Personéuses prayed and waited. Then came a sharp cold spell, and everything froze solid, including the avalanche. The men went down and cut a narrow trail over the top of that mountainous heap of solid snow so the dogs could pull the sleds over it.

On a clear, cold morning, the twelfth of March, the Personeuses set out for the coast. Most of the village came to see them off, giving them gifts of moccasins, hand-woven baskets, and other things they had made.

The fast sled was covered with bearskins and heavy blankets and padded with pillows for Mrs. Personeus and Byron, who sat at each end facing one another. The skins and blankets were wrapped around them and fastened securely to the sled with chains. No way could they possibly fall off the sled. Mrs. Personeus prayed silently that no rabbit would pop out of the underbrush.

The Yukon sleds had two handles in the rear like wheelbarrow handles that were used for pushing a heavy load. On the back of the sled was a little platform where the driver could stand and ride when the trail was good. Long poles along the sides were used in guiding the sled.

Their driver was a young Native named William. He shouted, "Mush! Mush!" and off they went. To turn left, he would holler "Haw!" and "Gee!" to turn right. The wooden sled bumped over the rough trail, jarring every bone. Even with the pillows and blankets for padding, a dog sled ride is far from comfortable. And Mrs. Personeus still had not recovered from her fall.

When they arrived at the avalanche, William felt it was too steep for the dogs, so he unchained his passengers and let them climb up over the huge mass of snow, while the men pushed and pulled to get their sled and the baggage sled up on the slippery trail. On the other side, Mrs. Personeus and Byron were again strapped in for the long, cold ride.

At first, the two sleds kept together, but gradually the faster sled pulled farther ahead. Soon the baggage sled, with Mr. Personeus and the other driver trotting along beside it, were left far behind and out of sight, as William kept calling, "Mush! Mush! Mush along!"

As they came around a curve in the road, they saw a huge, glistening mound of ice, where a small stream of water had been running across the road all winter, freezing in thin layers as it ran over the bank and cascaded 50 feet to the river below. The tops of some scrubby trees were sticking up through the ice along the bank.

As they neared the "glacier," William called to the dogs to stop. Then with a small axe, he began to chop a narrow trail over the slick mound, so the dogs could get a foothold. Even then, Mrs. Personeus did not like the looks of that slippery trail.

"Won't you unfasten these chains and let us walk over?" she asked.

William only answered, "I think I can get you across." Then, grabbing the handles of the sled, he yelled, "Mush! Mush along! Mush!" Valiantly, the dogs started forward.

Up they went on that gigantic icicle. Mrs. Personeus almost held her breath. Just as they neared the top, she saw the lead dog was slipping. He had missed the toe holds William had chopped, and began sliding toward the riverbank, pulling the next dog after him, and then the next one and the next. The dogs struggled hard to get their footing. The sled was now sliding at a tilt. William came up beside Mrs. Personeus and pushed the tipped sled along the side of the mound of ice, bracing his feet on the little branches of trees sticking up through the ice. Mrs. Personeus felt as though the sled were going to turn over and plunge to the river below. She reached out her hand and caught at a sturdy branch and pushed with all her might. Then she let it go and grabbed another as the sled inched forward, the driver holding it to the slippery slope.

Finally, the ice flattened out on the other side, and they were able to get on the trail again. Mrs. Personeus breathed a sigh of relief. Then the road dipped down nearer to the level of the river. Far ahead, they could see another, larger mound of ice across the road.

William said, "We go out on river now," and called to the dogs to turn off the road. Soon they were skimming over the frozen river.

The sun was shining brightly. The mountains towering on either side glistened a dazzling white in the sunlight. The vast stillness dwarfed the travelers, for there was no sign of human life in any direction, save for the lone sled.

Suddenly, the driver began to yell, "Haw! Haw! Haw!" But the dogs did not obey. Straight ahead they ran. William yelled again, louder than before. Still the dogs did not turn. He yanked the sled and yelled again, "Haw! Haw! Haw!"

Mrs. Personeus detected a note of fear in his voice. She knew that if a big, strong man felt fear, there must be danger somewhere, but she could not imagine what was frightening him.

William yelled frantically at the dogs a few more times. Then, with no word of explanation, he let go of the sled and ran toward the bank of the river.

Mrs. Personeus did not know what to think. She wondered what the dogs would do next. She knew they were fierce animals, part wolf and often treacherous, even attacking their own masters if they fell down in the snow. They were certainly no pets. She wondered what the dogs would do if they turned and saw the driver gone.

Are we at the mercy of these dogs? she wondered with dismay.

Then a still, small Voice whispered to her heart, "No, at the mercy of God." A sense of peace flooded her soul.

Little Byron asked, "Mama, where did William go? Why did he run away?"

"I don't know, dear," she answered, "but God will take care of us. Just pray."

Looking across the river toward the bank about a quarter of a mile away, Mrs. Personeus caught a glimpse of William trotting along. The dogs ran steadily onward for a mile or more. Then, not hearing the encouraging "Mush along!" they began to slow down. Suddenly, William was back, grabbing the handles of the sled and yelling, "Mush! Mush along!"

As they sped over the ice, Mrs. Personeus asked him, "Why did you leave the sled?"

"That thin ice," he replied. "Last week it all open water when thaw took thick ice down river. I try turn dogs from thin ice. They no go. Then I take my weight off sled; maybe they take you across. This old, thick ice now."

Mrs. Personeus silently thanked God for His care, but she shivered as she thought of being chained to that sled on thin ice. She hoped the dogs with the other sled would be more obedient, and that her husband would be safe.

As they neared the coast, the sun became quite warm. Far ahead, they could see piles of icebergs along the riverbank. Suddenly, Mrs. Personeus saw a long, black streak across the ice in front of them. As they drew nearer, she saw it was open water. The thick ice had a big crack across it, and the river ice was beginning to move out. She pointed it out to William.

"We can make it," he said.

When they reached the crack, the lead dog jumped across the two-foot-wide crack. The other dogs followed. The long Yukon sled bridged the crack quite easily with William's firm, guiding hand on the handles. As Mrs. Personeus looked down at the dark, swiftly flowing water, she suddenly felt very thankful that the thin ice a few miles back had held them.

Just then, they heard a terrible roar. Looking up, they saw an avalanche hurtling down the mountain toward the river. It leaped from cliff to cliff like a mighty waterfall. They were all watching it when suddenly the sled struck something and overturned.

Mrs. Personeus clutched the wooden brace on the upper side of the sled as it slid along on its side. Quickly, William grabbed the sled's handles and yanked, trying to lift it back on its runners. There was a sound of splintering wood, and one of the handles broke off in his hand. He ran to the side of the sled, took a firm grip, and lifted it upright on the runners again.

Mrs. Personeus had not made a sound. Quickly, William bent over the sled and looked at her. "You hurt?" he asked anxiously. "My mother tell me take good care of you."

Mrs. Personeus assured him that she was all right, only a little shaken.

Soon they left the river, and Mrs. Personeus was glad to be back on the road again. They reached Haines without further mishap, stiff, sore, and tired, but thankful to be safe. Friends welcomed them, and in a few hours Mr. Personeus arrived with the baggage sled. The next day they took the steamer to Juneau, thankful that the most dreaded leg of their journey was over.

In Juneau, the Personeuses repacked for the long trip to Pennsylvania. From Juneau, they traveled by steamer to Vancouver, British Columbia;

then over the Canadian Rockies by train, stopping in Winnipeg and Toronto; then into New York and Pennsylvania, to Mary Park's home in Soudersburg, arriving home just a few weeks before their baby daughter, AnnaMae, was born.

On May 28, Byron came down with a severe case of the measles. At two o'clock in the morning on May 29, AnnaMae was born in Mary Park's home. The next day Byron took a turn for the worse and nearly died, but the Lord spared his life in answer to prayer.

When AnnaMae was three weeks old, Mary observed, "Florence, you walk as though every step hurts you."

"It does," she replied.

"Well, there must be something wrong," Mary told her. "You should feel back to normal by now. I know of a good bone specialist in Lancaster. I want you to see him."

When the doctor had examined Mrs. Personeus, he stepped back and stared at her in amazement. "It's a marvel to me that you can walk at all," he said. "Your pelvic bones are broken apart and grate against each other with every step you take. You will have to go into a body cast for six months. Then you will have to learn to walk again."

Stunned at the prospect, Mrs. Personeus said, "I'll have to think about it," and hurried out of his office as fast as she could go—a painful waddle, as she later described it.

The next day was Sunday. As usual, the Personeuses attended services at the Lancaster Assembly of God. They told the congregation what the doctor had said. They told of the need for them to return to Alaska soon, since two older ladies were taking care of the work there.

Spontaneously, the people gathered around Mrs. Personeus to pray for her. And God completed the healing work He had begun in her body back in Klukwan. After church she walked home without a limp, free of pain for the first time since her fall six months earlier.

In just a few months the Personeuses were able to return to their beloved Alaska to continue the work in Juneau. They returned praising God, knowing that through her suffering more glory had been brought to the name of the Lord. If she had been healed instantly in January, they would never have known what a miracle God had performed.

Decker Way in Juneau in 1917.

**Inside the Personeuses' first home in Juneau
on Decker Way.**

The Mission on Front Street (S. Franklin) in Juneau (1918-24).

The fire next door to the Mission in 1918.

Traveling by horse-drawn sled from Haines to Klukwan on Jan. 13, 1922.

The Tlingit Indian village of Klukwan on the Chilkat River in April 1922.

The village of Klukwan (1922).

The congregation at Klukwan in 1923.

**The dog sleds loaded for the Personeuses' trip to the
coast in 1923.**

**The Chilkat River over which the Personeuses
traveled by dog sled.**

CHAPTER 14

"YOU HAVE TO MOVE!"

"Trust in the Lord with all your heart, and lean not on your own understanding; in all your ways acknowledge Him, and He shall direct your paths" (Proverbs 3:6).

In 1925, after seven years in the little mission on South Franklin, the Personeuses were shocked when they were informed that a businessman had rented the building out from under them by offering the landlord more money. He wanted to use the whole building, so the mission was asked to move.

For several weeks the little band of Christians fasted and prayed and looked for another building on South Franklin, but all the rents were too high. Discouraged because they could find no suitable place, they turned to the Word of God, where they learned a wonderful lesson from Psalm 42: "Why are you cast down, O my soul? And why are you disquieted within me? Hope in God, for I shall yet praise Him for the help of His countenance." With this reassurance from the Word, they began to praise the Lord and pray with more faith and assurance.

The next day the Lord directed Mr. Personeus to an empty building on Seward Street. It had been a drug store, then a theater. The windows were filled with theater billboards. This building, however, proved to be larger, lighter, better ventilated, and it was away from the beach so the tide did not come in under the building as it had done on South Franklin Street.

When the businessman began to remodel the building on South Franklin he had rented out from under the Personeuses, he discovered the standards supporting the building were rotten and almost ready to collapse. Realizing the condition of the building they had so reluctantly left, the Personeuses praised God again for His love and care for His own. If they had remained in that building, it might have collapsed under the weight of the next heavy snows.

Another benefit of the move was the location in a more stable part of town. The first years in Juneau had been discouraging in terms of trying to start a church. God had blessed and people had given their lives to

Christ, but the converts were transients who felt no responsibility for the work of the mission. Living expenses in Alaska were so high and conditions so primitive that people only worked for the summer months in Alaska. People could not afford the high cost of coal and wood needed for heat in the winters, and few houses were insulated. Every fall a mass exodus south occurred. And every fall the Personeuses had to start again to build up a congregation.

With the move to Seward Street, the Personeuses were able to reach a more stable part of the community. When people accepted Christ as Savior, they began to tithe and to work for the Lord in the church. The assembly began to grow.

One Sunday, a young draftsman who worked for the Bureau of Public Roads joined the assembly and became the organist. During an evangelistic meeting in 1928, the organist, Ivan F. Winsor, was baptized in the Holy Spirit. He became a faithful deacon and Bible teacher in the Juneau church, as well as organist-pianist, until 1939, when for health reasons he moved to Sequim, Washington, where he continued to work for the Lord.

Evangelist W. E. Day, a graduate of Glad Tidings Bible Institute, came to Juneau to hold evangelistic meetings. Several of the congregation received the baptism in the Holy Spirit, and several Filipinos surrendered their lives to Christ. Thus began an outreach to the many Filipinos who worked in Juneau.

CHAPTER 15

EVER INCREASING FAITH

"He sent His word and healed them" (Psalm 107:20). "In the name of Jesus Christ of Nazareth, rise up and walk" (Acts 3:6). "To another faith by the same Spirit, to another gifts of healings by the same Spirit" (1 Corinthians 12:9).

All along the Pacific coast in Alaska are many salmon canneries. These companies employed many Filipinos. In Juneau a large number of Filipinos also worked in the gold mines.

One day while Mrs. Personeus was visiting a sick woman whose husband was in jail, she witnessed to a young Filipino who was playing with the children. He began to attend the services at the Juneau mission and soon gave his life to Christ and was filled with the Spirit.

Cleto Bargayo, an open-hearted, good-natured young man, became a real witness for the Lord all along the Pacific coast from California to the Aleutians. He had never had the privilege of going to school, so he could not read and write. Wanting to learn to read the Bible, he began going to the Personeuses' home two nights a week for lessons in reading, writing, and arithmetic. With the Bible as his textbook, he also learned many spiritual truths.

Cleto longed to see his countrymen come to know the Lord. Not only did he pray for them, he kept witnessing to them and inviting them to services at the mission. After two years they began to come.

The first one to come was Cleto's roommate. One Saturday, the Personeuses were invited to Cleto's home to talk to the new convert about the water baptismal service planned for the next afternoon. Mr. Personeus explained that water baptism shows we are buried with Christ in baptism and raised to walk in newness of life.

A Filipino man in his forties was sitting quietly in the shadowed corner of the room, listening intently. When Mr. Personeus invited the new convert to the preparatory service for all the candidates in the Personeuses' home that evening, the older man stood and eagerly asked, "May I come too?"

95

The Personeuses learned he had just arrived in Juneau. Not knowing where to go, he had asked a Filipino on the street if he knew anyone who would help him get a job and a place to live. He had been directed to Cleto.

Aleppio Holmedilla drank in every word as Mr. Personeus told him about Jesus and the way of salvation. In simple, childlike faith he accepted Jesus as his Savior and Lord. Then he, like the Ethiopian eunuch of old, asked, "May I be baptized too?"

That next afternoon, at high tide, on the beach near the Bethel Beach Children's Home, Mr. Personeus baptized a Swede, a Mexican, a Chinese, and two Filipinos instead of just one. Although it was midsummer, patches of snow still gleamed white on the mountaintops around them. The water was cold, but their hearts were warmed by the love of God as they followed the Lord in water baptism.

Aleppio became another earnest witness for the Lord. He later came to board with the Personeuses in order to escape evil companions. Always courteous, good-natured, kind, and generous, he would say, "I've learned more of the Bible in four months in your home than I did in 40 years in the Catholic Church."

A lover of music, Aleppio often brought fine musicians home with him. After a musical treat, the Personeuses were privileged to share the Gospel with them. Aleppio gave a violin to Byron, who, with his musical talent, could pick up any instrument and play it in a very short time.

In 1925, the mission had more Filipinos than any other nationality in its congregation. Most of them left Juneau during a strike in the gold mines several years later. Many had accepted Jesus as their Savior and had been baptized.

One of these was Emil Bernaldes, a young man in his teens. After he became a Christian, he was eager to study the Bible, so the Personeuses started a Bible study group for young people. Desiring to escape evil companions and unable to find a suitable place to live, several of the young Filipinos became boarders in the Personeuses' home. In addition, Mr. Personeus was able to rent another house, which he divided into three apartments to sublet to Christian Filipinos.

One day as Emil was studying about Jesus, he suddenly asked, "Why don't some Pentecostal missionaries go to the Philippine Islands? I never heard about divine healing, or the baptism in the Holy Spirit, or about Jesus coming back to this earth again over in the Philippines."

Mrs. Personeus answered, "We don't know. Perhaps God will send you back to the Islands with the message."

He looked startled at the thought, shook his head, and replied, "Oh, I could never be a missionary to my people."

"Oh, yes, you could if Jesus calls you," Mrs. Personeus responded. "Let's pray that God will send someone to the Islands with the Full Gospel message."

Emil worked in the Alaska-Juneau Gold Mine as a rock picker. His job was to stand by a broad, moving belt where broken pieces of gray rock passed by him. If he saw any pieces that showed any white quartz in them, he was to snatch them off the belt. The gold was hidden in the white quartz. These rocks were then crushed into small bits to separate the gold from the worthless quartz.

As Emil was working one day, Jesus called him to leave the gold mill and carry the precious Gospel to his own people. Just as Jesus had called the fishermen to leave their nets and follow Him and He would make them fishers of men, so He called Emil to carry the Word, which is "more to be desired than gold," to his people. Emil went to Central Bible Institute in Springfield, Missouri, to study the Bible and prepare for the ministry. When he graduated, he returned to the Philippine Islands, where he laid down his life preaching the Gospel.

One evening as Mrs. Personeus hurried to get ready to go to the mission, everything seemed to go wrong, and she was late. But God had an appointment for her to keep. Just as she reached the door of the mission, a very small Filipino in a Navy uniform approached from the other direction. As he came abreast of her, to her surprise and embarrassment, she turned to him and heard her voice say, "You come in here."

He pulled his sailor cap from his head, bowed politely, and replied, "Yes, ma'am," and followed her into the mission.

He was a stranger to everyone, and Mrs. Personeus wondered why she had all but ordered him into the meeting.

Realizing he was in a church, he pulled the cigarette from his mouth, and sat down. Soon he was listening eagerly to the message from Luke 10:20: "Nevertheless do not rejoice in this, that spirits are subject to you, but rather rejoice because your names are written in heaven." Mr.

Personeus went on to explain the importance of having our names in the Book of Life and how to become a child of God.

When the altar call was given, the young man went down and gave his life to Christ. When he arose from the altar, he glowed with happiness. Then he told the Personeuses a strange experience he had had as a young boy.

"My mother was devout Roman Catholic in the Philippines," he said. "She wanted me to go to church, but I rebelled. Then I become very sick, and the doctor pronounced me dead. During the time he thought I was dead, I saw a beautiful pearly white gate. A man in shining white told me I could not enter because my name was not written in the Book. Then I felt myself being drawn quickly away to a vast valley filled with flames. Horrified, I cried out for mercy, and shortly thereafter, I found myself in my own room again."

He vividly described what he had seen. When they turned to Revelation 20:12-15 and read the verses that describe the Book of Life and the lake of fire, he got very excited.

"I've never read the Bible nor heard those verses before," he declared, "but that's true! That's true! I saw that Book! I saw the lake of fire!"

Grevacio continued, "After I recovered, I went to church and confession as often as I could, even after I joined the Navy during World War I. I asked every priest I met how I could get my name in God's Book. They told me the church roll was God's Book, but I knew there was a book in heaven that must have my name in it or else I would go to that lake of fire. This evening, I was on my way to confession, always hoping to learn more about that Book. When you said, 'You come in here,' somehow I knew I'd learn about the Book, and I'm so glad I found out at last!"

Another young Filipino who found Christ as his Savior in the Juneau mission was Peter Castro. A very ambitious young man, he was working in the gold mill and saving his money to go to Boston to study to be a doctor. But God had another plan for Peter's life and was calling him to take the Full Gospel to his own people back in the Philippines. Emil Bernaldes had already sent his application to Central Bible Institute, but Peter was undecided. The Personeuses felt a great burden of prayer that he would yield his life to God completely.

About this time, Mrs. Personeus began having spells of what she thought was acute indigestion. She and her husband would pray and praise the Lord until she had relief. Then the attacks began to come more frequently and with greater severity until she was afraid to eat anything. The pain was often so intense that she would ask her husband to drive her out of town in their car, so their children and boarders would not hear her screams of pain.

One day, she had a very severe attack and collapsed. Mr. Personeus carried her to the house and laid her on the couch. A number of Christians, including their Filipino boarders, gathered around to pray for her. She was conscious but unable to open her eyes or speak. She heard sobbing from a man close by. She tried to open her eyes, but could not, until she heard Peter Castro praying, "Oh, God, don't let her die! Don't let her die! I'll go! I'll go!"

Mrs. Personeus' heart was filled with joy, and she immediately began to feel better. As soon as she could open her eyes, Peter asked for the application for Bethel Bible School in Newark, New Jersey, where Mr. Personeus' brother Edgar was teaching. After Bible school, Peter went back to the Philippines as a missionary, where he ministered for many years, starting 25 to 30 new congregations and taking the Gospel to head hunting tribes in the mountains of northern Luzon. In 1958, he became the District Superintendent of the Northern Luzon District of the Assemblies of God.

After a short time, however, Mrs. Personeus had another attack and nearly died. Mrs. Costigan insisted they call a doctor.

When the doctor examined her, he said, "You have a very advanced case of gallstones. I can arrange for you to have an emergency operation, but you have only a fifty-fifty chance of surviving. In the meantime, I can give you morphine for the pain."

At the mention of morphine, Mrs. Personeus remembered people she had cared for while she was in nursing who had become addicted to the drug, so she refused to be treated.

"I would rather trust the Lord," she told the doctor.

"You're taking your life in your own hands!" he argued.

"No, I'm putting my life in God's hands," she replied. "If He wants to take me, I'm ready to go. But I believe Jesus can heal me."

The doctor walked to the door, shaking his head, and repeated, "You're taking your life in your own hands. The convulsions will become more severe until they end in death. You're liable to die any minute when the next convulsion comes."

A summer of suffering had passed, and it was now fall. Mrs. Personeus had lost 40 pounds that summer. Her faith began to waver. Discouraged and weak from the intense pain and lack of food, she despaired that she would ever be healed.

Calling her husband, she told him, "I don't think I can live through another of those awful convulsions. We might as well face facts. I don't think it is God's will to heal me." Then she told him some things she wanted him to do after she was gone.

"But isn't there anything I can do for you now?" he asked, heartbroken.

At first she said, "No, I guess not," but then she remembered a book they had ordered from an advertisement in the *Pentecostal Evangel, Ever Increasing Faith* by Smith Wigglesworth. She had been so sick she had not been able to read it. So she asked her husband to get it and read it aloud to her.

He sat in the doorway, reading by the light in the next room. As he read, their faith increased. He had not read more than 10 pages when suddenly the power of God fell upon him with a gift of faith. He jumped up, and with the authority and power of the Holy Spirit, ordered, "In the name of Jesus Christ, I command those gallstones to go! Woman, rise up and claim your healing!"

Mrs. Personeus got up out of bed for the first time in weeks and walked back and forth in the room, hands raised above her head while she praised God. For 10 minutes or more they praised the Lord together, while God removed the hard lump in her side. Though she lived another 60 years, she never had a recurrence, even though medical science tells us the body cannot dissolve gallstones. She had said with Job, "Though He slay me, yet will I trust Him." But God had sent His Word, quickened it to their hearts, and delivered her from death's door.

That night she had the first good night's sleep she had had in months. In the morning she began to eat and within a week had gained five pounds. She continued to gain in strength until her weight was back to normal.

CHAPTER 16

SIX MONTHS TO LIVE!

"These signs will follow those who believe: in My name...they will lay hands on the sick, and they will recover" (Mark 16:17, 18).

Mrs. Personeus soon had opportunity to share her testimony of healing with a young woman, a new neighbor of Mrs. Costigan. Helen Johnson had lost several babies before little Jean was born. Then complications had set in. Doctors told Helen she would never have another baby. Mrs. Costigan had witnessed to her and invited her to church, but Helen was not interested, until she developed a severe kidney infection and had to have a kidney removed. Lying on the operating table, she prayed that if God would spare her life, she would serve Him.

When Helen recovered, she forgot her promise to God, until she began to experience symptoms of another kidney infection. Frightened, she went to church with Mrs. Costigan. That night when Mr. Personeus gave the altar call, Helen Johnson went forward and gave her life to Christ.

Hearing the Christians at the mission pray in other tongues, she asked Mrs. Costigan, "What language are those people speaking?"

"Don't you know what that is?" Mrs. Costigan asked.

"No," Helen responded.

When Mrs. Costigan explained about the baptism in the Holy Spirit, Mrs. Johnson opened her heart to receive the infilling of the Holy Spirit, and she too began to speak with other tongues as the Spirit gave the utterance.

Shortly after her conversion, Helen went to the doctor. "Mrs. Johnson," he said, "I know you want to know the truth. Your remaining kidney is badly infected. Medical science has no treatment for it. You only have about six months to live." (In the 1930s antibiotics and the wonder drugs had not yet been discovered.)

Devastated, the young mother sobbed out her despair to God. "My husband is not a Christian. I have a little girl to raise. I see many dirty, neglected, unwanted children on the streets of Juneau. I wanted my child, and You are going to take me from her. It's not fair!"

101

The Lord directed her to Isaiah 54:1: "'Sing, O barren, you who have not borne! Break forth into singing, and cry aloud, you who have not travailed with child! For more are the children of the desolate than the children of the married woman,' says the Lord."

As she read that verse, the Lord spoke to her heart: "Open your life and your home to those neglected children on the streets of Juneau."

"All right, Lord. You know I'm dying, but if that's what You want me to do, I'll do it," she agreed.

When she expressed to her unsaved husband her desire to take in children, Lyle said, "You've had some dilly ideas in the past, but this is the dilliest. But, if that's what you want to do, I'll help you."

The next time Helen visited Mrs. Costigan, the older woman observed, "You seem blue today. What's troubling you?"

Helen blurted out her whole physical problem.

"Don't worry about that," Mrs. Costigan began.

"What do you mean, 'don't worry about that'? It's my life we're talking about!" Helen interrupted.

"I didn't mean it that way," Mrs. Costigan answered. "I was going to say you should ask Brother Personeus to pray for you to be healed."

"Healed?"

"Yes, Jesus heals today just as He did when He walked on earth." Then Mrs. Costigan, always ready to testify of what Jesus had done for her, told Helen how Jesus had healed her of a serious heart condition.

Later, Mrs. Personeus shared how the Lord had healed her and raised her up from the point of death.

About that time, Evangelist R. S. Peterson came to Juneau to hold revival services. During one of the meetings, Mrs. Johnson came forward for prayer for healing. As Brother Personeus and Brother Peterson anointed her with oil and prayed in faith, she was completely healed.

When Helen Johnson went to be with the Lord 40 years later, that one kidney was still functioning perfectly.

Shortly after her healing, Mrs. Johnson took a young girl into her home, Lillian Lorraine Lehtosaari. Her mother had died, and Lillian, although young, had been a dancer and performer with her father. When he tried to commit suicide, she went to live with the Lyle Johnsons. Lillian remained with them until she went to Bible school, where she met and married Alvin E. Capener. They ministered for many years among the Eskimos and Aleuts in Alaska, building the Assemblies of God churches at Nome, Point Barrow, and St. Paul Island, one of the Pribilof Islands in the Bering Sea.

Soon the Johnsons took in other children, until the burgeoning family outgrew their home. Mr. Personeus helped them enlarge it and build bunk beds for the children. This was the beginning of the Johnsons' Children's Home, later called the Juneau Children's Home, of which "Auntie" Johnson was the matron for many years until her death in 1967. Soon, Lyle, too, came to know the Lord as his personal Savior, and he worked faithfully right alongside "Auntie."

Edward Hughes was the oldest of several children abandoned by their father. Their mother was blind and deaf. Serving as her eyes and ears, Eddie would take her shopping and look after the younger children. Because they often stole just to meet some of the necessities of life, the Hughes children had a very bad reputation in Juneau. Many times Eddie heard parents yell at their children, "I don't ever want to see you with that Hughes boy again!"

When Eddie's mother became ill and had to enter the hospital, Eddie and his brothers and sisters were placed in the Juneau Children's Home. There, Eddie learned of Jesus and gave his life to the Lord. Later, he went to Bible school and then married Jean Johnson, Helen and Lyle's daughter. Edward Hughes pastored in Petersburg in Southeastern Alaska and then in California for a number of years before returning to Alaska to serve as pastor of First Assembly of God in Fairbanks, Alaska. He then served as the Assistant Superintendent of the Alaska District of the Assemblies of God for 14 years.

Another boy in the Juneau Children's Home who went to Bible school and entered the Full Gospel ministry was George (Jerry) McNevin. After pastoring in California, he too returned to Alaska to pastor Bethel Assembly of God in Juneau from 1974 to 1985 and continued to minister in Alaska until his death in a plane crash on his way to preach at a logging camp near Juneau.

Many lives have been changed by the power of God as the result of one little lady's witness to her neighbor of what God had done in her own life.

CHAPTER 17

TRUST AND MAKE THE BEST OF THINGS

"Commit your way to the Lord, trust also in Him, and He shall bring it to pass" (Psalm 37:5).

In the midst of the revival with Evangelist R. S. Peterson in 1929, their place of worship was again rented out from under them. This time the notice did not upset the congregation as much as before, even though they had less time to find another location. They had learned from their previous experience that God must have a better place for them. And He did.

A dance hall on nearby Main Street, which the Personeuses had often prayed would be closed, now stood empty. It had been a snare to many of the young people in Juneau. Then one night after a drunken fight at the dance hall, the Chief of Police had forbidden any more dances to be held there. Learning that the Personeuses were looking for a place to rent for their church, the owner offered them the dance hall for $25.00 a month if they would fix it up. Thus, the dance hall "got converted" into a Gospel lighthouse.

Larger, lighter, and more suitable than the previous place, the new location also had nine rooms upstairs. These rooms provided classrooms for the Sunday school. To make the place suitable as a house of worship, however, required a lot of hard work and elbow grease.

Soon, the Personeuses also moved into the upstairs rooms, which had previously been a rooming house. A long hall ran from the kitchen with its coal range at one end to the living room with a coal heater at the other end. The other rooms opened into this hall, but none of them were heated, except for the bathroom, which was warmed by the hot water tank. The building had no insulation, so when the Taku wind howled off the glacier, the family would find the water in the goldfish bowl frozen. Then, the only way to keep warm was to sit with their feet in the oven, and AnnaMae often did her homework atop the heater in the living room.

With larger facilities the Personeuses began holding Vacation Bible School for two weeks each summer. Many children of all ages attended.

In 1930, the J. Ernest Click family began attending the church. The father of three children, Mr. Click served as Sunday school superintendent until they left Juneau in 1939. Under his enthusiastic leadership, the Assemblies of God Sunday school in Juneau soon grew to be the largest Sunday school in town with well over 100 in attendance.

The Clicks had built a lovely home in Juneau and a log cabin on the beach at nearby Tee Harbor, which, along with the parsonage above the church, became the focal points for the social life of the church. Tuesday evening Bible study was held at the church. Cottage prayer meetings were held in different homes each Thursday evening. Friday evening was the young people's service. Everyone would come, but the youth were in charge. Before each service Mr. Personeus or Byron, when he was old enough, would drive their old seven-passenger touring car "out the road" and bring back a load of people for church. Sunday evenings before the service, they would conduct street meetings on a nearby corner. One evangelist, Mrs. Wade, could be heard blocks away when she spoke at the street meetings.

Radio came to Juneau in the early 1930s. Across the back yard from the church's new location, radio station KINY began broadcasting from the top floor of the five-story Goldstein Building. One Sunday, the station manager visited the church and Sunday school. He was so impressed with the singing and the orchestra that he asked their permission to put the last 15 minutes of the Sunday service on the air free of charge each Sunday. To do this, a microphone was dropped out the window of the radio station into the back window of the church. The Personeuses also paid for a 15 minute broadcast every Sunday afternoon.

One day, an old Indian woman stopped to see the Personeuses. "I just wanted to tell you how much we like to hear you on the radio," she said. "Every Sunday my old man and me just wait to hear Mr. Personeus' voice. Then we get on our knees and stay there all the time he talks. We thank God for the good words from the Bible. We live on an island where there is no church, but we listen to your church service. We want to thank you."

The Personeuses always practiced hospitality, even during the Depression years when food and money were scarce. Each Saturday Mrs. Personeus would cook a large meal for Sunday, the family's one good meal with meat for the week. Sunday morning she would look around the church to see if there were any newcomers or any who looked lonely or discouraged. These she would invite to dinner, and the large dining room

105

table was nearly always crowded. Yet, the Lord always seemed to stretch the pot roast or meat loaf so that some would be left over for several leaner weekday meals.

One day, a lady knocked on the door of the parsonage. Mrs. Parker from Strawberry Point (now called Gustavus), about 90 miles by boat from Juneau, was selling strawberries door to door. It did not take long for the Personeuses to discover that Grandma Parker was a Christian, and she very much wanted her family to come to know Christ as Savior. She invited the Personeuses to come to Strawberry Point and help her for a couple weeks each summer with the Sunday school she conducted in the schoolhouse, as well as pick strawberries for themselves. They soon became good friends, and the two families exchanged hospitality often. Mrs. Personeus noticed a motto on Grandma Parker's wall, which intrigued her and inspired her to write this poem:

TRUST, AND MAKE THE BEST OF THINGS

Do the skies seem dark and cheerless?
Former joys have taken wings?
Heart is heavy with forebodings?
TRUST, and make the best of things.

Life must have sunshine and shadows,
Winter's cold, ere new growth springs;
Sun and rain will bring the flowers,
TRUST, and make the best of things.

Careless words have oft brought sorrows,
Numbing pain, and torn heart strings,
But the Lord gives balm for healing.
TRUST, and make the best of things.

Lonely for old friends and places?
Days to which fond memory clings?
God is faithful. Just look forward,
TRUST, and make the best of things.

Jesus knew the Cross was waiting,
Taunts and shame and scourge's sting,
But He trusted God the Father,
TRUST, and make the best of things.

Every pain has compensation
For the heart that bravely sings,
While our faith grows daily stronger;
TRUST, and make the best of things.

For we know that God is planning;
He is working out all things
For the good of those that love Him;
TRUST, and make the best of things.

God is teaching us and training
For the glories Heaven brings.
Let us yield ourselves completely.
TRUST, and make the best of things.

—Florence L. Personeus

In 1937, the Reverend and Mrs. Watson Argue conducted an evangelistic campaign in Juneau. During these meetings the Sunday school broke its attendance records with 117 in Sunday school. The next year, 1938, Bethel Assembly of God was set in order by the Reverend Frank Gray, Superintendent of the Northwest District of the Assemblies of God, who was visiting Juneau on his honeymoon. Thirty-eight members signed the roster, and the Sunday school averaged around 100 in attendance. During the formative years many people had come to know Christ as Savior and had been baptized in water and filled with the Holy Spirit, but most had not remained in Alaska. The church was now not only viable, but also thriving.

Juneau, the capital of the Territory of Alaska, and its largest city at that time, had changed considerably in the 22 years since the Personeuses had landed there that cold, wet November evening in 1917. Then, on Front Street (now called South Franklin Street) along the waterfront all the buildings and even the boardwalk street had been built on piling above the beach, and the tide had gone in and out under them. By 1939, the beach had been built up with waste rock from the gold mill, and South Franklin Street was paved and full of automobiles. Many concrete office buildings and government buildings had been erected. Lovely homes and apartment houses, stores selling all the modern conveniences, and fine schools made Juneau a much more pleasant place to live. A steel suspension bridge had been built to span the 500-foot-wide Gastineau Channel, thus connecting Juneau with Douglas Island. People could now drive across the bridge instead of crossing the Channel on a small ferry.

Living expenses, however, were still extremely high. Food had to be shipped in. Soft coal, which burned rapidly, sold for $23.00 a ton. The more efficient hard coal was not available. When the bitter Taku winds blew off the glacier, it took a lot of fuel to keep warm in all but the best-built houses. Still, the population was increasing and stabilizing.

When the Personeuses had first gone to Alaska, their mission work had been under the supervision of the Foreign Missions Department at the Assemblies of God Headquarters. In 1921, Alaska had been made part of the Northwest District, which included Washington, Oregon, Idaho, Western Montana, and Alaska. Of course, this was before the age of modern airline travel, so Alaska was virtually cut off from any administrative assistance because of its distance from the rest of the Northwest District. In 1930, Alaska was again brought under the Foreign Missions Department, and Brother Personeus was appointed Field Representative for Alaska, a post he held until 1938, when Alaska came under the jurisdiction of the newly created Department of Home Missions of the Assemblies of God in Springfield, Missouri.

The Personeuses had taken no vacation or furlough in 16 years, so in 1939 they went to the States for a year. The Reverend Ralph Baker was asked to serve as pastor in the Personeuses' absence. He, however, refused to stay unless he was voted in permanently, so the Personeuses did not return to Juneau after their furlough. Though they were disappointed, they characteristically accepted the situation as one of His appointments.

In 1940, John I. Conn, a deacon and charter member of Bethel Assembly, donated the corner lot on Fourth and Franklin Streets for the construction of their own church building on the very corner where the Personeuses had prayed their first night in Juneau in 1917. Until 1928, the

Conns' apartment house had stood on that site. A disastrous gasoline explosion in 1928 had destroyed their apartment house. Mrs. Conn had been using gasoline to dry clean some clothes. Their son Ivar and AnnaMae Personeus had been playing in the kitchen but had left the Conns' apartment just moments before the explosion. Mrs. Conn was killed in the fire, and Mr. Conn had been severely burned while trying to rescue his wife. After the fire, the Personeuses and Mrs. Costigan had helped Mr. Conn raise his motherless son.

With a building of its own, Bethel Assembly of God continued to grow and prosper.

**Congregation at Bethel Pentecostal Assembly on Seward
St. in Juneau in 1926. Notice how large windows are
braced with 2x4s to withstand the Taku winds.**

**Congregation of the Juneau Assembly on Main St. in 1932. Mr. Click,
Sunday school Superintendent, standing next to Rev. Personeus at
left.**

**The Personeus Family with pianist and helper
Ivan Windsor in 1936.**

The congregation of the Juneau Assembly in 1938.

**VBS in Juneau in 1938. The Personeuses
are just in front of door.**

The Personeus Family with Julia Costigan at the dock in Juneau.

CHAPTER 18

FAMILY REUNIONS

"I hope to come to you, and speak face to face, that our joy may be full"
(2 John 12).

The 16 years between furloughs had brought about numerous changes in the Personeuses' families back East.

When George N. LeFevre had disowned his children for becoming missionaries, he had forbidden his wife to see them. Refusing to follow his wishes, she arranged to see them as often as she could. Because he made life so miserable for her for seeing the children, she finally moved out of the family home. On December 31, 1925, Florence's eldest brother, Lincoln LeFevre, died in Lancaster, Pennsylvania. He had remained on the farm and tried to follow his father's wishes, even to the point of not marrying the girl he loved. On his deathbed he had tried in vain to bring about reconciliation between his proud, stubborn father and gentle, loving mother. Florence often said she felt Lincoln died of a broken heart.

Just two years later, Carl's older brother Edgar, who had been teaching at Bethel Bible School in Newark, New Jersey, after his return from a missions term in Liberia, was suddenly stricken with diphtheria and died two days later on November 1, 1927. He left a wife and three tiny daughters.

In March 1930, Florence had dreamed one night of her mother. In the dream her mother was in heaven with Jesus and free from all the cares and heartaches of this life. About six weeks later, Florence received word that her beloved mother had died of a stroke on March 8, 1930. Florence was devastated. For weeks she mourned her, sometimes even questioning God. Why had He called her to Alaska so she could not even attend her own mother's funeral? When she finally accepted her mother's death, she realized God had offered a great source of comfort in allowing her to dream of her mother in heaven. She could have prevented weeks of anguish if she had accepted the comfort of that dream immediately instead of allowing herself to become so agitated and full of self pity.

In 1932, Florence's eldest sister Anna, home on furlough from Chile, South America, visited the Personeuses in Alaska. They took her to the Mendenhall Glacier and even climbed the 3,576-foot Mt. Juneau. Anna was the sister Florence had looked up to all her life, so this was a very special time for her. As they visited together, Florence related to Anna an unusual experience she had had.

"One night the Lord awakened me and told me to get up and pray for you. Several times I started to get up from my knees, but the Lord impressed me to keep praying. Finally, the burden lifted. What happened on that date?"

"I remember it well," Anna answered. "The Catholic priests had ordered several men to kill all the Protestant missionaries. Ordinarily, I would be home before dark, but that particular night I was out late delivering a baby. It was very dark as I walked home alone. As I approached a wooded area through which the path passed, I felt myself suddenly lifted off my feet and whisked through the woods, though I saw no one. A few days later, a man came to me and told me how he and several other men had been waiting for me on either side of the path in the woods that night. They had been clutching knives with which to kill me, but they had been immobilized when they saw two large men in white clothing escort me swiftly down that path. Realizing my God had protected me, that man told me he wanted to serve my God too."

Anna also told of her miraculous recovery from black smallpox, though her lovely face was scared for the rest of her life. The doctor had pronounced her dead, but she said, "During that time I felt myself floating above my bed, yet I could see my body lying on the bed. I was lifted higher and higher until I saw a brilliant light. In that light I saw Jesus reach out His hand to me. I knew I would go to be with Him forever if I put my hand in His. But then I thought of the people of Chile who still had not heard of a Savior who loves them, and I said, 'But Lord, what about these people?' Then, without a word, He raised His hand over me in blessing. Then next thing I knew, I was back in my body. The amazed doctor said I had been dead for half an hour."

In 1935, Prohibition was repealed with terrible consequences in Juneau, as in the case of one drunk who staggered into the little mission on South Franklin. Before he left, though, he had surrendered his life to Christ and been delivered from alcohol by the power of God. Later, Jim

Murray went east to visit his daughter in Boston. When the Great Depression swept the country, Jim found work on a farm in Strasburg, Pennsylvania—the LeFevre farm! He told Florence's father all about the work the Personeuses were doing in Alaska. "You ought to be proud of your daughter," he scolded.

Jim had been sleeping in the barn, but when the snow came, Mr. LeFevre invited him to stay in a room at the house—his way of showing Jim he was liked in spite of his scolding.

Shortly before the Personeuses left Juneau for their second furlough, AnnaMae suffered from acute mastoiditis and nearly died. She could hear her parents on the telephone calling Christians to pray for her, but unable to move or speak, she could not respond to them in any way. She knew she was dying.

Then, suddenly, in answer to the prayers of God's people, the pain left. She felt wonderful! Her parents, however, would not let her out of bed. When her friends would come to her room to see her, they would gasp and ask, "Doesn't it hurt?"

Puzzled, AnnaMae waited until everyone had gone to church. Then she crept out of bed to get her hand mirror. When she glimpsed herself in the mirror, she began to laugh until the tears rolled down her cheeks. The side of her head was swollen out like a chin with her ear perched on the end of it. No wonder everyone gasped when they saw her. Instead of becoming upset over her strange appearance, however, AnnaMae took her mirror back to bed with her and hid it under the covers so she could peek at her funny-shaped head and laugh. Within a week the swelling had gone down, and she looked normal again. She had, however, permanently lost the hearing in that ear.

When the Personeuses arrived in Pennsylvania, after leaving Byron at Central Bible Institute in Springfield, Missouri, they learned that Florence's 90-year-old father was in the hospital. She had not seen him in 25 years. He had forbidden her to visit the family home, but she viewed his hospitalization as an opportunity to see him again.

In the 25 years since Florence had last seen her father, her hair had turned from blonde to snow white. As she approached his bed, he asked, "Do I know you? You look familiar."

115

Time had not softened his attitude toward her, though. When he finally learned who she was, he turned his head to the wall and would not speak to her again. He did, however, take quite a liking to AnnaMae, then 16, in spite of the fact that she was quite outspoken with him. Perhaps it was that very quality that endeared her to him.

He would say, "AnnaMae, don't be a bad girl like your mother."

She would respond, "I hope I can be half as good as she is."

Soon George LeFevre was well enough to leave the hospital, but the doctors would not allow him to return to his home where no one was available to care for him. His eldest daughter Anna was also home on furlough from Chile. She was living in a house in Lancaster that had been willed to George LeFevre's disinherited girls by their Aunt Salome, who had been a missionary to India. Not knowing that the Personeuses were living with Anna at the time, George asked Anna if he could stay with her until he was well enough to return to his own home. The Personeuses decided to move to Mary's, another of Florence's disinherited sisters, and George moved in with Anna.

Knowing how her father still felt about her, Florence and her family no longer visited Anna. Finally, Anna said, "Florence, this is our home. Papa has no right to make you feel unwelcome. I want you to come to dinner. I'll talk to Papa, so don't worry about him."

Anna had always had a way with her father. Even though he had disowned her for going to the mission field, they had been reconciled. So, when she told him about the dinner invitation, he listened.

The evening came for the Personeuses' visit. George dressed in his best suit. When Florence arrived, he took her arm ever so politely and seated her by himself. For the entire evening, however, though he was attentive and the perfect gentleman, he treated her as though she were a total stranger!

George never did ask forgiveness for disowning Florence, but she was allowed to visit the family home again. When her father died four years later, at the age of 93, Florence learned that she had been reinstated in his will, though most of his estate had been left to the LeFevre Cemetery and Historical Society he had founded. The Old Mill Stream Museum in Lancaster County, Pennsylvania, contains many items from the LeFevre estate, including the printing press on which Florence learned the printing trade.

In the Boston area in 1939, while itinerating to raise financial support for their ministry in Alaska, the Personeuses stayed in a home in Quincy, Massachusetts, where a young lady was boarding. She was away on vacation at the time, but the family with whom she lived told the Personeuses her unusual story:

Evelyn had been born in Alaska. Her mother had fallen off a dock and drowned when Evelyn was two years old. Unable to care for his little girl while he worked, her father had placed her in the home of a childless couple in Juneau, the Petersons. They became quite attached to her and kidnapped her. Taking her to Massachusetts, they had raised her as their own daughter. Evelyn believed the Petersons were her real parents until the day she heard them arguing. Mr. Peterson referred to her as "that Dahl kid." Later, as Mrs. Peterson was dying, she told Evelyn the truth about her parentage.

Hearing the story, the Personeuses were amazed at the providence of God. Evelyn's father had come to their mission in Juneau, heartbroken after the disappearance of the Petersons with his little girl. He had died without ever seeing Evelyn again or knowing what had happened to her. He had, however, given his life to the Lord before he died.

In 1946, the Personeuses, on furlough again, met Evelyn. How thrilled she was to learn she would meet her father in heaven!

In 1940, Byron graduated from Central Bible Institute, so the Personeuses, still on furlough, were able to attend the ceremonies.

That fall, when the Personeuses were ready to return to Alaska, Brother Fred Vogler, the chief executive officer of the Division of Home Missions at the Assemblies of God Headquarters in Springfield, Missouri, asked them to go to Ketchikan. The Coast Guard had a large station there, and nearby Annette Island was being fortified. Many servicemen were in the area, and the struggling mission in Ketchikan desperately needed their help.

CHAPTER 19

MOM AND POP

"You shall rejoice before the Lord your God, you and your son and your daughter, ...and the stranger and the fatherless...who are among you, at the place which the Lord your God chooses to make His name abide"
(Deuteronomy 16:11).

In 1940, Ketchikan, Alaska's southernmost city, was its second largest. Known as the fishing capital of the world, it stretched four or five miles along the north shoreline of Tongass Narrows, on Revillagigedo Island. At first glance, Ketchikan appeared to be sliding off the mountainside into the water. Its docks and business section were built on piling over the heaving tidewater. Like Juneau in 1917, its waterfront street was made of heavy planks on piling. The residential section was built up the mountainside, with steep streets and in some places, stairways.

Hundreds of fishing boats were moored to wooden floats (floating docks), which extended for more than two miles along the shore. More salmon was canned in Ketchikan's ten canneries than in any other city in the world. Boatloads of halibut were brought in to the cold storage plant and frozen for shipping. Lumbering was also an important industry, and Ketchikan's waterfront sported a large sawmill.

Ketchikan, like Juneau, had become modern in every respect by 1940. The city owned its own light, water, and telephone systems. Modern houses, hotels, and stores made living there very convenient. Yet, the city abounded with bars, dance halls, movie theaters, and gambling halls—places which helped to pull people down to destruction. The Personeuses found few churches there to help people find a saving knowledge of Jesus.

In 1935, Mrs. Josephine Gilmore had started a mission on Ketchikan's waterfront. Many transients had come to know Christ as Savior, but the work had not grown. Its poor location in an old storefront on the waterfront was one reason. The building was not conducive to starting Sunday school, which was the best means of growing a church then. Only three people were attending the mission when the Personeuses arrived in Ketchikan in the fall of 1940.

Mr. Personeus and Byron left Mrs. Personeus and AnnaMae in Pomona, California, for that first winter. AnnaMae had contracted a slight case of tuberculosis, and the doctors recommended she not go back to Alaska until spring.

In January, Mrs. Personeus was suffering intense pain from some complications of influenza. She tried to pray but was in such pain she could not think to pray. About this incident she later wrote, "Jesus spoke to my soul, saying: 'You can say the prayer I taught my disciples.' As I started, He gave me this poem. As I wrote it down, the pain left. I was healed."

Here is the poem she wrote that day, dated January 8, 1941:

PRAYER AND MEDITATION

OUR FATHER, precious words that Jesus taught,
Revealing to us such a God of love,
With the tenderest pity of a father,
Faithfully watching o'er us from above.

OUR FATHER, WHICH ART IN HEAVEN so fair;
Dwelling in realms of glorious light,
So loved this world, with its sin and its woe,
His only Son came from that Home so bright.

HALLOWED BE THY NAME, O Father!
Sacred and dear to each child of Thine,
The name of the Lord is our strong tower,
Holy and precious, O Lord divine!

THY KINGDOM COME, our hearts are crying.
Then wars and tumults all shall cease,
Then truth and righteousness shall triumph,
And all the earth be filled with peace.

THY WILL BE DONE, for it is holy.
Thy will, Thy plan is always best,
Teach us to love Thy will more fully,
Yielding our own, and thus find rest.

THY WILL BE DONE, IN EARTH AS IT IS IN HEAVEN
Where angels love to do Thy will,
That men shall bow in full obedience to Thee,
And righteousness the earth shall fill.

GIVE US THIS DAY OUR DAILY BREAD,
That we may have strength to do Thy will,
Spirit and soul and body must be fed,
And Thou alone, O God, my every need can fill.

FORGIVE US OUR DEBTS, AS WE FORGIVE OUR DEBTORS,
Yea, more, O Lord, do we Thy pardon crave.
We need Thy cleansing, and kind, forgiving spirit
Toward others, since Jesus died our souls to save.

AND LEAD US NOT INTO TEMPTATION,
As we travel through this world below;
There's sin and darkness all around us,
Give us grace and strength to meet the foe.

BUT DELIVER US FROM EVIL, Father,
Guard us safely day and night,
From sickness, accidents, dread disasters,
Most of all, from sin's dark blight.

FOR THINE IS THE KINGDOM, O blessed thought,
And Thou shalt rule o'er land and sea.
Thy people of every tribe and nation
Shall bow the knee someday to Thee.

AND THE POWER AND THE GLORY, Lord,
Are Thine forever more, and then—
We will worship and adore,
And give Thee all the glory, AMEN.

—Florence L. Personeus

Shortly after arriving in Ketchikan, Byron obtained a job as an announcer on the local radio station, which broadcast to the surrounding islands as well. The Personeuses were again able to preach the Gospel to those in isolated areas via a weekly half-hour Gospel program. They continued to hold services in the mission in the old storefront and lived in the one-room apartment at one end of the building, which contained two additional apartments rented to some drunks. When the Personeuses learned the community had a jail, they also began holding weekly services there.

When Mrs. Personeus and AnnaMae arrived in Ketchikan in the summer of 1941, they found living in the one-room apartment to be very difficult. The 12- by 24-foot room was still unfinished, with bare boards and two-by-fours showing. One corner had been partially partitioned off for a toilet and washbowl, the only source of water they had—cold water! Mr. Personeus had partitioned off one corner of the mission as a bedroom for Mrs. Personeus and AnnaMae. He and Byron slept on the couch in the room that also served as living room, dining room, study, and kitchen.

Since wallboard cost too much, they came up with an ingenious solution for covering the bare boards. Mr. Personeus brought home large cardboard cartons, which they opened out flat and tacked to the two-by-fours. Then they applied pretty wallpaper over the cardboard, which brightened the room considerably.

The building that housed the Ketchikan Gospel Tabernacle was built on piling right over the water. High tides lapped at the floor, forming icicles in the winter. It was impossible to keep feet warm in the winter. Mrs. Personeus suffered each winter with chilblains in her feet and legs.

One good thing happened that next spring. The drunks vacated the other apartments in the building the church rented, so the Personeuses were able to rent the entire building. No more drunken brawls would interrupt their sleep at night. And they now had a real bathroom with a bathtub!

In 1941, the Home Missions Department at Headquarters gave the church $400.00 to purchase two lots at $200.00 each on which to build its own house of worship. The lots were still wooded—full of trees, logs, huge stumps, and dense underbrush. Don Groves (who had come to Alaska as a civilian conservation corpsman and had come to know Christ as his Savior in Juneau under the Personeuses' ministry there) helped the Personeus men clear the lots in preparation for construction. Once the lots were cleared, Brother Fred Vogler, head of the Home Missions Department in Springfield, Missouri, came to conduct an open air ground-breaking service. The building program, however, ground to a halt when the United States entered World War II, because the necessary building materials became impossible to obtain.

On December 7, 1941, as the jailer let the Personeuses out after the jail service, he told them the terrible news that Pearl Harbor had been bombed. Overnight, life in Ketchikan changed. Since everyone was afraid the Japanese would bomb or invade Alaska, blackouts were a common occurrence. Mr. Personeus was appointed to be an air raid warden. Byron and AnnaMae attended compulsory first aid classes.

After Pearl Harbor, many more servicemen poured into the area. The Ketchikan Gospel Tabernacle was located near the USO, so Byron made a sign: "SERVICEMEN WELCOME! COME IN!" Before long, the men were coming and going almost around the clock as word circulated that here was a home away from home. Many dedicated their lives to Christ, and later, some even entered the ministry. Everyone began calling the Personeuses "Mom and Pop." Once again the Personeuses had found "His appointment" for their lives. After the war, Mrs. Personeus maintained regular correspondence with "her boys," even sending cards on their birthdays, until she could no longer see well enough to write—when she was in her nineties.

AnnaMae graduated from high school in Ketchikan in 1942 and attended Northwest Bible Institute in Seattle for two years. The summer of 1943, AnnaMae brought two girlfriends home with her from Bible school. AnnaMae and Dorothy White (now Dr. Dorothy DeBoer) had to return to school in the fall, but Margaret Reed had already graduated, so she remained in Ketchikan to help the Personeuses. When Pop asked her to preach one Wednesday in October, Mom told her she could invite anyone she wished to come for dinner that evening. While working at the USO, Margaret had met one Coast Guardsman whom she was sure was a born-again Christian, but she had not been able to get him to come to the Ketchikan Gospel Tabernacle.

Bob Cousart was a licensed Methodist preacher. Influenced by the testimony of George Beverly Shea, who later joined the Billy Graham Evangelistic Association, Bob had dedicated his life to Christ at the age of

19 at a "Higher Life" Conference at Keswick Grove, New Jersey, where Bev Shea was the featured soloist. When Bob came home from the conference that weekend, he had told his mother, "I got saved!"

"Saved from what?" she asked. "You've always been a good boy."

Soon, God began to deal with him about going into the ministry. "But I can't speak in public," he protested to the Lord.

As a seventh grader Bob had been president of the French Club. When they had presented a puppet play in French, it had been his responsibility to introduce the play. He had carefully written out what he would say on note cards, but when he had stood up to speak, the spotlights had blinded him so he could not read what he had written. Dumbly, he had crumpled the notes, dropped them on the floor, and run off. Hidden behind the puppet stage, however, he had recited his lines letter perfect.

But the Lord wouldn't take "no" for an answer. Bob finally yielded, and "taking himself by the scruff of the neck," as he later recalled the experience, he enrolled in a public speaking course at Temple University in Philadelphia. When the United States entered World War II, Bob had interrupted his studies for the ministry to join the Coast Guard.

The Methodist minister in Ketchikan had warned Bob to stay away from the Personeuses and the Ketchikan Gospel Tabernacle. But when Bob discovered that the Methodist pastor did not believe in the Virgin Birth of Christ, he began attending services at the chapel on the base instead. When Margaret invited him to a home-cooked dinner, however, he could not resist. Once there, he was too polite not to attend the service following the meal, at which Margaret was to speak. Thus, Bob found himself in his first Pentecostal meeting. He enjoyed it and continued to attend. Mom Personeus extended a double welcome to him when she learned he was from Philadelphia, near her home in Pennsylvania.

Thanksgiving dinner at the Personeuses' in 1943 was served in two sessions—half the turkey one night and the other half the next night—since only part of the group of servicemen could be present on any given night. The boys stationed on nearby Annette Island could only come to Ketchikan for a few days each month, but the rest had every other night off. Almost every evening the Personeuses' home was full of servicemen sitting around reminiscing about home, discussing Scriptures, or talking about the Lord. Others played games, read, played the phonograph, or teased the girls. Mom and the girls baked continually to keep the cookie jar filled. Each evening refreshments were served, and they had a time of devotions before the boys left by one o'clock in the morning for the base or the USO.

When AnnaMae came home for Christmas that year, she noticed handsome Coast Guardsman, Bob Cousart. He had been calling her parents "Mom and Pop" long before he had met her. He was engaged, however, to a girl back home.

As a baby, Bob had been baptized by sprinkling, but as he studied the Bible to discover for himself if the Pentecostal doctrines were really scriptural, he soon realized he needed to be baptized by immersion. Never knowing when he might be suddenly transferred, Bob and his buddy, Harold Kelly, asked Pop Personeus to baptize them in water. On a cold mid-January day, the icy Tongass Narrows, that arm of the Pacific Ocean on which Ketchikan perched, became the scene of a baptismal service as Bob and Harold followed their Lord in water baptism.

As Bob spent his spare time studying the Bible and seeking the Lord, he felt God was calling him to be a missionary. When he wrote to his fiancée about this, she broke their engagement. She had been prepared to be a Methodist minister's wife, but the life of a missionary was more than she bargained for. Soon Bob began corresponding with AnnaMae, who had returned to college. When Margaret Reed married Frank Tetro on June 1 (The Tetros later spent many years in Japan as missionaries.), Bob and AnnaMae were partners in the bridal party. They began going together that night.

In wartime, courtships progressed rapidly. Three weeks later, Bob proposed to AnnaMae. It was his night to be on duty, but he could stand the suspense no longer, so he asked another fellow to fill in for him. He met AnnaMae as she got off from work and walked her home, explaining that he needed her help in practicing the song he was to sing the next Sunday. In the sanctuary he asked her to marry him. As they re-entered the living room, he asked, "Are you happy, Pop?" When he answered "yes," Bob turned to Mom. "Are you happy, Mom?" She answered a puzzled "yes." Bob turned to AnnaMae. "Are you happy, AnnaMae?" When she answered "yes," he exclaimed, "So am I! Good bye!" and rushed out the door to return to his post.

"What was that all about?" Mom and Pop asked AnnaMae.

"He just asked me to marry him, and I said 'yes,'" she answered.

The next evening Bob came back to officially ask her parents for her hand in marriage.

A few weeks later Byron wrote that he was engaged to marry Marjory Thomas of Bremerton, Washington, a student at Northwest Bible Institute. His dream was to operate a mission boat in Southeastern Alaska. Realizing he could not earn enough money on his own to finance the purchase of a suitable boat, he had left Ketchikan in the early spring to itinerate by motorcycle in the Northwest District of the Assemblies of God to raise money for the project. Northwest Bible Institute served as a focal point for his itineration.

During the war engagements were often short. Not knowing when Bob might be suddenly transferred, he and AnnaMae were married by her father on August 16, l944, in a beautiful ceremony at the Tabernacle.

December 15, Bob was transferred back to Philadelphia, taking AnnaMae with him. The day they sailed away was a sad one for Mom and Pop. They wondered when or if they would see them again.

Arriving in Seattle, the Cousarts spent a few days visiting Byron and Marjory before they had to catch the train for the East Coast. Seeing the happily married newly weds, Byron and Marjory, who had planned a June wedding, decided to get married right away, on December 29, much to Mom's disappointment. She had planned to surprise them by attending the wedding in June.

In Ketchikan, new boys took the places of those being transferred out. To each one the Personeuses were Mom and Pop. On May 11, 1945, the Christian servicemen still in Ketchikan held a banquet for their friends who had helped to give them a home away from home. Mom and Pop Personeus were given the seats of honor. By June, Byron had obtained his missionary boat, the *Fairtide II,* and he and his new bride sailed into Ketchikan.

After the war had ended and the boys had all returned to their homes, the Personeuses turned their attention once again to building a church on the land that had been bought and cleared for that purpose. Since funds were needed in order to build, Headquarters recommended that the Personeuses return to the States to itinerate again.

One spring morning in 1946, a group of their friends gathered at the dock to say good bye to the Personeuses. As the boat pulled away from the shore, they had no idea that they would not be returning to Ketchikan to build that church.

Their itineration allowed them to once again visit family and friends, as well as several of "their boys." Florence was thrilled to be able to visit with her brother Charles and his family, who were home on furlough from Chile, South America. Thirty years had passed since she had last seen this brother, who had led her to the Lord. On Christmas Eve, 1946, Mr. Personeus received word that his mother, Flora Ellis Personeus, at the age of 90, had gone to be with the Lord. Thankful to be close enough to go home, the Personeuses drove to Bridgeport, Connecticut, for the funeral.

The Personeuses were visiting with Bob and AnnaMae Cousart and their first grandchild, AnnaLee, at Green Lane, Pennsylvania, where Bob was completing his preparation for the ministry at Eastern Bible Institute, when the Personeuses received word from Headquarters that they could not return to Ketchikan. It was January 13, Mr. Personeus' fifty-ninth birthday, and they had all gone to Lancaster to her sister Mary's home for dinner and to pick up their mail. Bob Cousart recalled the hurt the Personeuses felt when they learned they could not return to erect the church they had been raising funds to build. The pastor who was filling in for them had been voted in as permanent pastor. He would be the one to erect the church building in Ketchikan. They were stunned, but once again they characteristically swallowed their disappointment with a smile and, substituting an "H" for the "d," looked for "His appointment" in the situation.

When Byron and Marjory learned that the folks would not be returning to Ketchikan to pastor, they asked them to join them in their mission boat ministry in Southeastern Alaska. Returning to Alaska in 1947 after the birth of their second grandchild, Robert Paul Cousart, on January 30, the Personeuses became part of the boat ministry with their son and soon found "His new appointment" for them.

CHAPTER 20

THE BOAT MINISTRY

"Sing to the Lord a new song, and His praise from the ends of the earth,
you who go down to the sea, and all that is in it, the coastlands, and you
inhabitants of them...Let them shout from the top of the mountains. Let
them give glory to the Lord, and declare His praise in the coastlands"
(Isaiah 42:10-12).

During their years of ministry in Southeastern Alaska, the Personeuses had learned of many tiny fishing communities and canneries scattered among the islands of Alaska's "Panhandle." Most of these towns had neither churches nor Gospel witness of any kind—towns like Kake, Angoon, Hoonah, Tenakee, Pelican, Elfin Cove—accessible only by boat or seaplane. A mission boat was needed to carry the Gospel to these needy islanders.

At the close of World War II, Ralph Harris, newly appointed director of the National Youth Department at Headquarters, devised a plan he called "Speed-the-Light," in response to the Assemblies of God's missions goals for the postwar years. Through the Speed-the-Light program, Assemblies of God youth around the nation raised funds for the purchase of equipment needed by missionaries to speed the light of the Gospel to a sin-darkened world.

In 1945, funds from Speed-the-Light, together with the money Byron had raised itinerating, made possible the purchase of the *Fairtide II,* a gasoline-powered cabin cruiser, as a mission boat for use in Southeastern Alaska. Byron Personeus, with his wife Marjory, skippered the boat. During the summer months, they lived on the boat and sailed from island to island taking the Gospel to the many isolated villagers and cannery workers. In the spring of 1947, Byron's parents joined them in this ministry.

This unfinished poem, found written by Florence Personeus on the back of a used envelope, describes the scenes they saw as they sailed on the *Fairtide II.*

A ship rode gracefully thru the waters
Amid Alaska's green-clad isles;
On every side arose the mountains
Up from the water for many miles.

Dark against the sky they stood
Except for the snow-trimmed peak,
All clad in cedar, hemlock, and spruce—
Wood, waiting there for men to seek.

Along the shores of an island ahead
I saw an Alaskan fishermen's town
With canneries and fishing boats by the water's spread,
For salmon canning, 'twas a place of renown.

Out on the shimmering, gleaming waves
Fishermen captured the silvery horde,
Then to the canneries, from inlets and bays,
The salmon in cans were quickly stored.

Above the quivering waves below,
Along the shores many buildings stood
Supported by strong logs of wood
Like mighty trees in a forest grow.

Once in a dark and mossy glen
These trees had lived and grown,
But they were chosen by a master's hand
To work for others—they were not their own.

Chosen by him, prostrate they fell,
Yielding their members, from twig to limb,
Brought through the woodland to water's edge,
Bound in a raft, made ready for him.

Then to the place of service they moved,
They were lifted, and stood erect again
Along the beach near a rocky shore
Where a pile driver pounded them deep, and then

They stood up straight and strong once more,
Ready to serve in the world of men,
Holding up buildings, docks, and store,
Unmentioned by word or pen.

And then one day, after many years,
My ship drew near that same old shore.
The buildings, canneries, and wharves were there,
Upheld by those wooden pillars as of yore.

But the tide had gone far out to sea,
Leaving the beach quite high and dry,
Exposing the whole of those logs to me
And what had happened as the years went by.

Time and tide and many hard storms,
Barnacles, starfish, and the boring…

—Florence L. Personeus

Sailing in Southeastern Alaska can be very hazardous in times of storm—as Paul the Apostle described in 2 Corinthians 11:26: "In perils in the sea." Many times the Personeuses identified with his words in Acts 27:29: "We prayed for day to come." One time they lost their way in a dense fog and ended up among several small, rocky islands in perilous waters. But the Lord kept them from hitting any rocks. Many ships wrecked in Alaska's treacherous waters, and many lives were lost. For that reason, Psalm 107:23-31 came to have special meaning for the Personeuses.

Those who go down to the sea in ships,
Who do business on great waters,
They see the works of the Lord,
And His wonders in the deep.
For he commands and raises the stormy wind,
Which lifts up the waves of the sea.
They mount up to the heavens,
They go down again to the depths;
Their soul melts because of trouble.
They reel to and fro, and stagger like a drunken man,
And are at their wit's end.
Then they cry out to the Lord in their trouble,
And He brings them out of their distresses.
He calms the storm,
So that its waves are still.
Then they are glad because they are quiet;
So He guides them to their desired haven.
Oh that men would give thanks to the Lord for his goodness,
And for His wonderful works to the children of men.

One time when the Personeuses were taking a boatload of missionaries and church workers to a convention in Juneau, the boat hit a submerged log. They did not realize that damage had been done to the hull. A violent storm blew up and several boats larger than the *Fairtide II* sank. But God carried them safely through. After returning the workers to their homes, Byron put the boat in dry dock to see what damage had been done. When he touched the spot where the log had hit the hull, his hand went right through it.

Sailing up Chatham Strait, between rugged spruce and hemlock clad mountainous islands, the *Fairtide II* drew near a large salmon cannery. Byron slowed the engine and began to play a hymn over the boat's public address system. As the strains of "Let the Lower Lights Be Burning" wafted across the waters, cannery workers paused to listen. One familiar hymn after another reminded the workers of the love of God and their need of a Savior. Children and adults began to gather on the dock as the *Fairtide II* drew closer. When the boat had reached the float and was securely tied up, several Natives asked, "Will you hold a church service for us in our community hall tonight?"

The next day the *Fairtide II* carried the Personeuses to yet another cannery or small town scattered among the thousands of islands that make up the Alexander Archipelago. Although the senior Personeuses had come to Alaska 30 years before, they had not realized how vast the mission field was among these islands of the "Panhandle."

At one small town, several Natives, who had come to know Christ as their Savior years before in Juneau, came aboard with tears in their eyes. They were experiencing severe trials, and their faith had almost reached the breaking point. Hearing the hymns floating across the waves, they thought it was music from heaven. They knew God had sent help in their time of need. The Personeuses ministered to them, praying for one of their children who was sick. The Lord touched their child and gave them joy and victory in their souls once again. Then the couple helped to arrange a meeting place for the Gospel service that evening.

At another of the salmon canneries, the Personeuses were given permission to hold the service in one of the cannery warehouses. The night air was chilly, and it had begun to rain. Wide cracks in the warehouse walls allowed the cold wind to blow in the dampness. The place had no seats of any kind. Stacked against the walls were rows of the low, flat trucks used for stacking the crates of canned salmon. The Personeuses arranged these trucks in rows for pews. They were low, rough, splintery, and none too clean, but they were better than nothing. The rain began to fall harder, and they wondered if anyone would come. Byron began to play his accordion, while his father played his trombone. Soon, most of the "pews" were filled. Groups of men stood along the back. The cannery superintendent from Seattle and his family came also. Marjory led the singing while her mother-in-law handed out hymnals. They had a good service that night, and the next night more people came. During the afternoon, the Personeuses shared a flannel graph Bible lesson with the children. When they had to leave to sail on to other islands, the people asked, "When will you come back for more services?"

At another cannery the captain of a boat at the dock, with tears in his eyes, told the Personeuses how he had once loved the things of God back in the States, and how glad he was to hear the good old hymns again. Then he asked, "Have you been to Pelican, over on Lizianski Inlet? That is a place that really needs the Gospel. They have no church of any kind there."

Wherever they went, the Personeuses found people who were hungry for spiritual things and their meetings were usually well attended. And in several villages, people asked, "Have you been to Pelican?" Then they would add, "That's a place that needs the Gospel."

The *Fairtide II* sailed on toward Chichagof Island. When they reached Elfin Cove at the entrance to Lizianski Inlet, they were told the inlet was shrouded in fog. They waited a day, and still the fog had not lifted. Then they began to pray that God would clear the fog away, so they could enter the inlet and reach Pelican. The fog billowed ahead, but as the boat drew near, it lifted and cleared.

The Personeuses soon learned that the reports about Pelican had not been exaggerated. They found a very rough town with no church, no law, two or three taverns, a community hall, a schoolhouse, a salmon cannery, a saw mill, and a cold storage plant that handled tons of fresh fish each day, brought in by hundreds of fishing boats. The town was strung out for a mile or so along the cliffs. The houses were built on either side of the long boardwalk, all built on piling 10 to 15 feet above the narrow beach at the foot of the cliffs, so the tide could come in and out under them. The boardwalks had no railings at that time, and drunks frequently fell off as they staggered from bar to bar. One drunken fisherman fell off and landed on an anchor abandoned on the beach below. Seeing one prong sticking up between his arm and side, he wondered how he could still be alive with an anchor through his body. The Personeuses' first night in Pelican a man was stabbed just two boats down from where the *Fairtide II* was tied. Pelican certainly needed the Gospel.

As the *Fairtide II* approached Pelican and the Gospel music wafted out over the waves, people stopped to look and listen. Some remarked, "I've never heard anything like that in Pelican!"

One Native couple, Mr. and Mrs. Roscoe Max, hearing the Gospel music, hurried down to the float to welcome the Personeuses. Roscoe, an Eskimo from Barrow, Alaska's northernmost tip, had come to Sitka, the former Russian capital of Alaska on nearby Baranof Island, to get an education. There he had become a hopeless alcoholic until God had saved him and filled him with the Holy Spirit. Two years earlier he and his wife had moved to Pelican to work in the cold storage plant. They had been holding Sunday school and prayer meetings wherever they could and had been praying for a Full Gospel church in Pelican. They were thrilled to meet the Personeuses.

That evening after playing hymns and announcing the service over the boat's public address system, the Personeuses went ashore to hold their first Gospel meeting in Pelican at the community hall, a huge scow (a building built on a barge) tied up along the boardwalk. The Personeuses had learned that a committee in Pelican had been working to get the Presbyterians to build a church there. This committee, having been present in the service, sent Mrs. Laveda Klippert as their spokesperson to the *Fairtide II* to see the Personeuses.

"Will you help us build a church in Pelican and provide a pastor?" she asked. "If you will, then we will drop our request to the Presbyterians. But we must know that we can count on you. Many children are growing up here that need the influence of a church."

The Personeuses promised to pray about their request.

The next evening (Friday), a teen dance was scheduled for the hall, so the Personeuses and the Maxes met at the home of Mrs. Marie Mork for a prayer meeting. Mrs. Mork too had been a hopeless alcoholic until she gave her life to Christ and was baptized in the Holy Spirit.

That night the little band of Pentecostal Christians asked the Personeuses, "Will you help us build a church in Pelican? We need a church, and we want it to be Assemblies of God."

Saturday evening another dance was held at the community hall, so the Personeuses "broadcast" a Gospel message over their public address system in the harbor where many fishing boats docked while unloading fish and purchasing supplies.

Sunday morning, while his father cleaned the community hall in preparation for the church service, Byron "broadcast" another service from the boat, reminding people that Sunday was the Lord's Day and announcing the services to be held at the community hall.

The place reeked of liquor and tobacco, but the community hall was the only place available for a service. And the Personeuses were made even more aware of the need for a church that afternoon as about 40 children gathered for the Sunday school they conducted.

The Personeuses could see that Pelican had children growing up with no spiritual influence in their lives. They began to pray that if God wanted them to build a church there, He would set His seal of approval on the project by giving them the salvation of one person in the evening service.

When the altar call was given, not one, but two, young fishermen came forward for salvation. In view of God's confirmation that evening, the Personeuses agreed to do all they could to help build a church in Pelican. But they had no funds available, only faith in God that He would answer the many fervent prayers of His people.

The next morning the committee showed the Personeuses a building site they could have for a church on the condition that they would clear it and erect the building. The site was on a hill above the cold storage plant, overlooking the inlet, where a church would stand as a lighthouse to every boat that sailed up Lizianski Inlet to Pelican. But the land was covered with gigantic stumps and "windfalls"—layers of fallen trees, often as many as seven deep, piled up like a giant game of "pickup sticks." It would take months of back-breaking work just to clear the land—blasting and sawing large stumps, half rotten logs, and windfalls, and digging out roots.

After looking over the land, they decided they would come back in the fall to begin the work, hoping by then to have help. But when they prepared to leave Pelican to continue their itinerary among the islands, a Bendix spring broke, and they were unable to start their boat engine for three weeks while they waited for parts. They spent those days working on the building site during the day and holding services in the evenings.

The city fathers recommended that they build living quarters in the church, since Pelican was experiencing growing pains, and no place for them to live was available. While they were building the church, all four Personeuses lived on the *Fairtide II*, in very cramped quarters. The boat was only a summer yacht, and in the winter months it was almost impossible to keep warm. They all suffered from rheumatism. Drying clothes was impossible because of the dampness. The bedding mildewed. Their shoes and books turned green with mold. And the boat rocked and bounced in the stormy weather.

The float where the boat was tied and the boardwalks were very slippery when wet, which was most of the time. One evening, Florence Personeus slipped and fell, hurting herself quite painfully. Her husband helped her back to the boat and prayed for her. None of them realized how badly she had hurt herself until she tried to turn over in her sleep. She cried out with pain as she felt a broken rib buckle up under her hand. Pelican had no doctor or nurse, but the Great Physician was there. Calling on the Lord, she lay on her back, took a big, painful breath, and stretched the broken rib straight again. For a day or so she stayed flat on her back, keeping her lungs filled with air, until the rib was knit. And the Lord took care of it.

CHAPTER 21

CHURCH ON A HILL

"Many are the afflictions of the righteous, but the Lord delivers him out of them all" (Psalm 34:19).

During the summer months Pelican was a bustling little community, with hundreds of fishing boats bringing loads of fresh salmon and halibut from Icy Straits and the Gulf of Alaska. In addition to a salmon cannery, Pelican had a cold storage plant that handled tons of fresh fish—cleaning, salting, freezing, and packing them for shipping on freighters. When winter set in, however, activity ground to a standstill.

With no power tools, it took the Personeuses until November to clear enough land and to gather enough materials to begin to build. An old logger whom they had befriended 30 years before had supplied them hand tools with which to work, but no bulldozers were available to push away the windfalls and stumps. They did it all by hand.

Then, when they tried to secure a building loan from Headquarters, they found too many other churches ahead of them asking for loans, so the Personeuses prayed and wrote letters, and God supplied the needs in many ways. Churches in the States sent offerings. On one occasion, a contractor, who had finished a project with supplies left over, sold them to the Personeuses at cost. When the architect said it would cost $400.00 to draw the plans, Byron drew them for nothing. And they were able to use some secondhand items that were in good condition. The town could not promise them water or electricity, so Byron figured out a way to get water to the church and to the house just beyond them as well. He also put in a septic system for the building.

The only way to haul the building materials and cement to the building site on the hill was with a handcart or wheelbarrow. What could not be hauled in the cart or wheelbarrow had to be carried up on their backs.

All through the winter the two men, assisted by their wives, toiled with the building. Often, they found their work covered with snow and ice in the morning. The snow had to be shoveled and was soon piled higher than their heads. Progress was slow and discouraging. Many times the work was hindered by lack of finances, and necessary materials were often unavailable, since all supplies had to be shipped in.

In spite of the bad weather and back-breaking toil, by January 1948 they had erected the framework of the 24- by 40-foot church with living quarters and three large bedrooms. In March, Brother Fred Vogler came from Headquarters in Springfield, Missouri, to see how the building was progressing. He was very surprised to see the framework up. By spring, the building was entirely enclosed, although the finishing asbestos shingles had not yet been added. Even before the interior finishing had been completed and the heating system installed, the Personeuses began using the church for services.

Having a place to meet without interruption was a blessing. They had been holding services at the community hall, but with one hall to accommodate meetings of all kinds, it was far from ideal. One time, the Personeuses announced a special evangelistic meeting to be held in the community hall in the early part of the evening. Then, a meeting of the local longshoremen's union was scheduled to begin at 9:00 o'clock. While the evangelist was still preaching, the union men walked in and began their meeting. The church people had to close their service rather abruptly.

In addition, the community hall was more like a barn than a house. The walls consisted of just one thickness of boards nailed to two-by-sixes, and the beating rains came through the cracks between the boards. The place was impossible to heat in the winter. And it often reeked so strongly of liquor and tobacco, the Christians could hardly stand to breathe, let alone sing.

That summer, the Cousart family returned to Alaska from Pennsylvania, when Bob finished Bible school. With another man to assist in the building, the work progressed more quickly. Bob helped the Personeus men haul sand and gravel from a creek three miles away for the cement chimney. AnnaMae had to keep their small children in snowsuits all summer because of the cold winds that blew into the unfinished living quarters.

That fall, AnnaMae began experiencing difficulty in her pregnancy with their third child, so the Cousarts had to move to Juneau. They were living in Mrs. Costigan's basement apartment, but they needed money for doctors and the hospital. They had planned to return to Pelican as soon as the baby was born, but the only job Bob could find was at Alaska Coastal Airlines, and he had to promise to stay for at least one year. Late the next summer, when Miss Peterson, matron of the Bethel Beach Children's Home (which the Personeuses had started following the 1919 flu epidemic), died of a stroke, Mrs. Krogh and the Personeuses asked the Cousarts to take over the operation of the home. Bob continued to work at the airlines as boss of the cargo department to support the home. AnnaMae had her hands full with thirteen children, nine of them under five and two babies in cribs, with no additional workers.

Alaska Coastal Airlines operated a fleet of amphibious aircraft throughout Southeastern Alaska. The villages and cities of the "Panhandle" were accessible only by boat or pontoon planes landing on the water. One of the benefits of Bob's job was free airline transportation for the entire family, so the grandchildren frequently visited Pelican. The Personeuses were always happy when AnnaMae's three children, AnnaLee, Paul, and Kathy, visited.

Mrs. Personeus, by then in her early sixties, had decided that flying was more than she could handle. The boat trips around the islands had been bad enough, but to fly through thin air was more than she cared to experience. She was too old to fly, she thought. But one day as she put AnnaLee, her eldest but still preschool-aged grandchild, on the Grumman Goose and saw her sit trustingly in the cockpit with the pilot who would deliver her to her father, she thought, "If that little child can put so much trust in her father's wishes, then I must overcome my fear of flying and trust my Heavenly Father to take care of me." Since then, Mrs. Personeus has flown all over Alaska and the continental United States many times. She wrote this poem as a tribute to the Alaska Coastal pilots:

GOD BLESS THE PILOTS

God bless the brave men who pilot the planes
Over the mountains, straits, inlets, and bays,
When weather is fair, and oft when it rains
And clouds hang low on dark, gloomy days.

Over the mountains, capped with snow,
Densely covered with hemlock and spruce,
Then circling, glides to the waters below,

Startling the sea gulls, ducks, or wild goose.

Into some lonely Alaskan bay,
Or an inlet, where people watch and wait
For the welcome plane that brings the news,
Perhaps some passengers, mail, or freight.

Then off with a roar, and up in the air,
To other places, lonely and small,
On rugged islands or isolated shore,
Where people wait for the plane to call.

Or, speeding away on some mercy flight,
Where someone is sick, or injured sore,
Carries them safely through dimming light,
So they can reach some hospital's door.

A hunter is lost, a boat in distress,
Agonized hearts wish they can be found.
Brave pilots face dangers, join in the search,
Scanning the waters, also the ground.

Alaska's coasts are rugged and wild,
With storms and winds, and snow and rain.
It is not always pleasant to fly,
But, what would we do without the plane!

Our pilots need courage, wisdom, and skill,
A keen, clear eye and a steady hand,
Flying in summer's fogs, and winter's chill,
Bringing the planes safe back to land.

"God bless the brave men who fly through the air,
Protect them, and keep them from harm,
Take care of the pilots," is often my prayer,
As they soar away in a storm.

For 'tis only God who has all power,
And in His great love, has sent His Son
Who can save, and keep in every hour,
Giving peace, when the last flight is done.

—Florence L. Personeus

The Personeuses completed the interior of the living quarters over a period of years as money became available. The temporary steps to the upstairs bedrooms were made of pieces of shiplap. In January 1949, Mrs. Personeus fell from the top step, landing near the bottom with her left foot doubled under her on the sharp edge of the shiplap. As she lay there, the words of Psalm 34:1 came to her mind: "I will bless the Lord at all times; His praise shall continually be in my mouth." She began to praise the Lord as her husband and son carried her to her bed and prayed for her.

That evening, they carried her downstairs for the prayer meeting. As the Christians prayed for her, she felt as though a large, warm hand were being laid on the injured leg between her knee and ankle. She got up and was able to walk a little, but her foot and ankle remained badly swollen, so for a few weeks she stayed off her feet as much as she could. By March, her left foot was still badly swollen and all colors of the rainbow. About halfway between her ankle and knee was a large blood clot, an inch wide and three inches long. But she was walking.

The first week of May, Mrs. Personeus made a trip to Juneau. As a neighbor was saying "goodbye," she slipped some money into Mrs. Personeus' hand saying, "Will you please go to the clinic in Juneau and have an X-ray taken? I'm worried sick about your leg."

When she went to the clinic, three X-rays were taken. As she waited for the doctor to give her the results, she noticed two doctors in the next room looking at her X-rays with puzzled expressions on their faces.

Her curiosity stirred, she called out, "May I see them?"

The doctor pointed out the white lines where the bone had been broken in two places. The lower break had been badly splintered. He said, "You can see where the bone was broken, but it is perfectly straight. There is nothing more we can do."

"Praise the Lord!" she exclaimed.

He looked at her curiously before responding, "Yes, you can thank God. You were fortunate the skin didn't break. If it had, you might have bled to death. Instead, the blood went into your foot. That's why it is so swollen and discolored."

Then the other doctor said, "But look at that blood clot. It should be cleaned out. There is danger of infection."

But her doctor cautioned, "She has gone three months and no infection has set in. If we cut into it, we might start a running sore. Mrs. Personeus has good, clean blood, with no alcohol or nicotine in it. I think we'd better leave it alone."

The other doctor said, "But look at her foot. She shouldn't be walking on it."

Her doctor replied, "If she wants to walk on it, let her walk. Not many would try, but it will stimulate the circulation."

In His own way, God had again taken care of Mrs. Personeus.

CHAPTER 22

"BUT YOU'RE NOT OLD!"

"The Lord has done great things for us; whereof we are glad"
(Psalm 126:3).

In 1949, due to the high cost of gasoline, the *Fairtide II* was sold in order to buy a larger, diesel-powered boat, the *Taku*. Each summer Byron and Marjory continued their boat ministry, but the senior Personeuses remained in Pelican to pastor the church they had built there. On July 3, 1950, Brother Fred Vogler and Brother Gayle F. Lewis from the Assemblies of God Division of Home Missions in Springfield, Missouri, came to Pelican to dedicate the church building to the Lord's use. It was completely debt free.

The senior Personeuses ministered extensively to the many children in the community. Because of the frequent visits of their grandchildren, the Personeuses soon became "Grandma and Grandpa" to the other children as well.

Many of the little ones who lived on the south end of town were not able to walk the mile or so to get to the church at the other end of town. Since the only vehicles in town were a Jeep fire engine and a tiny Crosley car, Grandpa came up with a unique "bus" for transporting those children to Sunday school. He had obtained the job of meeting all the Alaska Coastal Airlines planes to load and unload all the mail, packages, and baggage. These were hauled to and from the post office, which also served as the airlines office, in a large two-wheeled cart, which measured about three feet wide, five feet long, and three feet deep, with two sturdy handles on it for pushing heavy loads. He would borrow this cart, every Sunday morning, rain or shine, summer or winter. About an hour before Sunday school, he would ring the big bell, which hung in the church belfry; then he would play a recording of carillon chimes playing hymns over the church's public address system. When the bell rang and the hymns wafted out over the town, the children would know it was time to get up and get ready for Sunday school. Then Grandpa would push the empty navy blue mail cart down the boardwalk to the other end of town to

142

collect the children. The little ones would pile into the cart, which Grandpa would push, while the older ones would walk along beside. As they walked along, children would join them all along the way. After the morning service, they would return home the same way. How those children loved Grandma and Grandpa!

One evening the Personeuses had invited her Sunday school class of junior boys and girls to the house for a party. Before serving the huge chocolate cake and whipped strawberry Jell-O, Grandma played the games right along with the children. Finally, she straightened up and said, "Whew! I'm not as young as you all are. I'm going to have to rest."

"But Grandma," said 10-year-old Joe incredulously, "you're not old!"

And even into their nineties Grandma and Grandpa weren't old. They were always young at heart, interested in young people and open to new ideas. And today many of the children they ministered to are serving the Lord because Grandma and Grandpa showed them the love of Jesus. One of their greatest joys was to receive letters from some of the children who had grown up and were still serving the Lord.

Grandpa loved to entertain children with his clowning. What a variety of expressions he could make with one face! The children would howl with laughter. Grandma would say, "Oh, Carl, stop it!" Then she would gather them around her and tell them the Bible stories that were so precious to her or read aloud from books she had loved as a child. Best of all was her recounting of the adventures of her childhood or of their early days in Alaska.

Every morning, Grandma and Grandpa would read their well-worn Bibles together, even when grandchildren were visiting, and then pray long and earnestly for God's guidance in their work and in the lives of their loved ones and friends. The grandchildren wiggled and squirmed, but each one read and prayed in turn—from the eldest to the youngest.

Grandma spent many nights keeping up with her correspondence. After a long day and the visiting grandchildren had been put to bed, she would sit in her room and write letters until the early morning hours. She corresponded regularly with several hundred people, servicemen and transients they had ministered to throughout their ministry, as well as family and friends. In addition to her beautifully handwritten letter, she would include a poem she had written or a Gospel tract. In spite of her late hours, she would be one of the first to get up in the morning and with a cheery "good morning," greet each grandchild as he or she came down the stairs.

Grandma never seemed to speak a harsh word nor was she ever too busy to listen to a problem or lend a helping hand. She told her grandchildren, "Live for **J**esus first, **O**thers second, and **Y**ourself last. That's the way to spell **J-O-Y**."

In spite of the active pace of their lives, Grandma found time to grow things. Her home was always full of plants. She often taught her grandchildren the names of them—the scientific names as well as the common ones. One lady, after caring for Grandma's plants for a week while Grandma was out of town, asked her, "Did you know you have more than a hundred plants? I quit counting when I got that far." Every summer she also planted a vegetable garden with lettuce, radishes, carrots, beans, as well as a myriad of flowers. The children especially loved her strawberry pyramid.

The snow-capped mountains rising high on the other side of Lizianski Inlet form the only barrier between Pelican and the Pacific Ocean. When the moist air off the ocean hits those mountains, it condenses, making rain. And in the winter it snows—huge mountains of snow. It seemed Grandpa was always shoveling snow, trying to keep the walks up to the church clear. He worked for the town shoveling snow from all the boardwalks on the north end of town from 1948 to 1958. Sometimes he would have to throw the heavy snow higher than his head.

One evening after shoveling snow fast and hard, Grandpa had what they thought was probably a heart attack. He and Grandma were all alone, and Pelican still had no doctor. Fearing that he would not live through the night, they prayed and praised the Lord for victory throughout most the night. By morning, he felt well and strong again. He went on shoveling snow, even into his nineties.

After living in Pelican for some time, Grandma began experiencing severe pains in her left arm and hand when she walked up steps or up the hill to the church. The pain often became so severe she had to stand still until it eased. One day, as she was waiting for the pain to ease while walking up the hill, she met the nurse who then lived in Pelican. Grandma asked her why her arm and hand hurt so badly.

"That's a bad sign," the nurse told her. "The next time you get to Juneau, you should tell the doctor about that."

Grandma did as the nurse had recommended.

"You have symptoms of a serious heart condition," the doctor explained. "I want you to take it easy, and stay off hills."

"But I live on a hill!" she protested.

"Then you'd better move," he told her. He prescribed some little white pills, saying, "Carry these with you at all times. Take one whenever you have those pains. And stay off hills!"

But Grandma prayed about it. She told the Lord she couldn't move off the hill, and there were no cars to drive her up the hill, so He'd just have to take care of her heart. And she never had to take even one of those little white pills. She never had another pain from her heart, which remained strong until the day she died at 96 years of age.

During those years in Pelican Grandma had noticed a lump growing in her right breast. She didn't give it much thought until it began to get larger and become quite painful. Then she requested special prayer and was anointed with oil. The lump spontaneously ruptured and gradually began to shrink until it was completely gone. But it left a large scar. Finally, she asked a doctor to look at it.

"When did you have surgery?" he asked.

"I have never had surgery," she replied. "The Lord shrunk that tumor."

"That's a miracle," he exclaimed. "May I call another doctor to look at it?"

And three doctors declared it to be a miracle.

Life in Pelican, though a small town, was seldom dull. Chichagof Island abounded in brown bears, which were extremely dangerous. Reports of brownies mauling humans were heard from time to time. Bears were sometimes sighted around Pelican. One day the nurse was carrying an oxygen tent along a path around the point from the main part of town. Hearing footsteps ahead of her on the rough trail, she called, "Yoo-hoo! Wait up!" hoping she could get some help carrying the equipment. The footsteps ceased, so she hurried around the bend in the trail—and almost ran into the hug of a big brown bear towering upright above her in the path! Dropping her oxygen tent and bag, she pivoted and ran screaming back the way she had come. Fortunately, the bear did not give chase, for a brownie can easily outrun a human.

With so many fishing boats sailing in and out of Pelican, it was inevitable that some would be wrecked in the treacherous waters outside the protection of Lizianski Inlet. One boat with three men aboard foundered in a terrible storm on Yakobi Rock in Cross Sound. One of the men somehow managed to scramble up on the rock, but the other two were lost when their skiff was swamped. The storm raged for several days. With each rising tide, the rock was submerged in the swirling, near-freezing salt water, soaking his legs. As the tide ebbed, exposing the rock, his legs became encased in ice. For three days he clung tenaciously to that rock. For three days he prayed, "God, if You will get me off this rock alive, I'll serve You." When hope seemed totally gone, he was rescued. But both of his feet had to be amputated, as well as parts of his fingers and ears. When he learned to dance on his artificial legs, the whole town cheered. Sadly, however, he forgot his promise to God. As far as is known, although he lived for many more years, he died without making things right with God.

One fishing family that had two boys decided to make Pelican their year-around home. The parents claimed to be avowed atheists. The boys were tough and full of mischief, especially the youngest. One time, he threw a match into an empty oil drum. The boom ricocheted from cliff to cliff. Fortunately, no one was hurt. Another time he threatened to blow up the church, and he had the dynamite! A year or so later, during a summer Vacation Bible School held by the Personeuses' daughter, AnnaMae, Gary gave his heart to the Lord. For several years he attended Sunday school and church faithfully, even in spite of threats and beatings. Sometimes his older brother would come and drag him out of the church in the middle of a service. A very intelligent boy, Gary often asked challenging questions about Christianity and the faith, and seemed to be quite argumentative, until the Personeuses and Cousarts learned he was asking the questions his parents used to try to convince him his salvation was a hoax. Unfortunately, his parents' influence eventually won out. In 1967, he horrified the nation when he kidnapped Barbara Mackle, a Florida heiress, and buried her alive in the Everglades in a coffin-like box he had constructed, equipped with a limited air supply and a small amount of food.   Fortunately, she was rescued.   He spent many years in a penitentiary.   Though he is now free, to our knowledge, he has still not returned to the One who can truly set him free.

The day in May when the fishing boats began to arrive from the Seattle area and the Filipino cannery workers flew in each spring, Pelican came to life. The population numbered only about a hundred in the winter months, but on the Fourth of July it grew to about five hundred. The trolling boats, after spending about 10 days out on the fishing grounds, would return to Pelican to unload the salmon iced down in their holds and restock the boats with food, fuel, and ice. The church was the first sight that greeted them as they sailed up the inlet. Many fishermen visited the Personeuses or attended the services when they were in port. As a familiar boat would sail around the point, the Personeuses would grab their ever ready binoculars to verify the name on the bow. The fishermen often waved as they sailed by. One fisherman, Peter Moe, who came to know Christ as his Savior in Pelican, accompanied the Personeuses as their "chauffeur" on a furlough they were able to take in 1956.

In 1956, the *Taku,* Byron's third mission boat, was lost to the Assemblies of God. Offerings for the boat ministry had dropped off due to the Korean War, so Mr. G. A. Barum, of Puyallup, Washington, had been financing the boat ministry and had purchased the *Taku* for that purpose. When Mr. Barum died suddenly before he had the opportunity to change his will to leave the boat to the Assemblies of God, Mr. Barum's heirs took over the *Taku*. Without the mission boat, Byron and Marjory were free to fill in at Pelican while the senior Personeuses took their furlough. When the Senior Personeuses returned to Pelican in the spring of 1957, Byron and Marjory were then asked to pastor the church at Cordova.

**Personeus Family in living quarters of Ketchikan
Gospel Tabernacle (1942).**

**Mr. Personeus at the pulpit inside the
Ketchikan Gospel Tabernacle.**

"Mom & Pop" Personeus with "their boys" in Ketchikan in 1943.

The banquet for the Personeuses given by the Christian servicemen in Ketchikan in May 1945.

**Sunday school on back of porch of Ketchikan
Gospel Tabernacle c. 1945-46.**

The Charles C. Personeuses aboard the *Fairtide II*.

The 65-ft. mission boat *Taku*.

Carl and Byron Personeus hauling lumber from the
sawmill to the site of the Pelican church.

The church at Pelican.

The church at Pelican overlooking the Inlet.

**AnnaMae and the grandchildren visit
Grandma at Pelican (1949).**

Meeting the plane at Pelican (1950).

Bringing the children to Sunday school.

The Sunday school at Pelican.

A Sunday school picnic in back of the Pelican church.

Shoveling snow at Pelican.

CHAPTER 23

GOOD FRIDAY EARTHQUAKE

*"God is our refuge and strength, a very present help in trouble. Therefore
we will not fear, though the earth be removed, and though the mountains
be carried into the midst of the sea; though the waters roar and be
troubled, though the mountains shake with its swelling" (Psalm 46:1-3).*

In 1958, at the age of 70, the Personeuses decided it was time for them
to retire. They asked their daughter and son-in-law, the Cousarts (who had
given up the children's home due to AnnaMae's health), to come and
pastor the church in Pelican. The Personeuses moved back to Juneau to
the little cottage left to them by Mrs. Costigan, who had gone to be with
the Lord in 1955. While they were fixing up the little house, their dear
friend from the early days in Juneau, Mrs. Femmer, invited them to live in
her basement apartment where they had been living when their first child,
Byron, was born.

Their story does not end here, however. To the Personeuses, the word
retire meant "putting on a new set of tires and taking off again." Free of
the responsibilities of pastoring, they began visiting churches around
Alaska, speaking where invited, helping with needs, and being a blessing
wherever they could. When the Cousarts moved to a new pastorate in
Seward in 1960 so their children could attend high school, the Personeuses
returned to Pelican to fill in until the new pastor arrived. Then, when
Byron and Marjory were invited by the Pentecostal Assemblies of Canada
to take over a boat ministry on Vancouver Island in British Columbia, the
senior Personeuses flew to Cordova to fill in there for six months. Soon,
they were filling in all over Alaska for missionaries going on furlough.

Elmer Ignell, a contractor and long-time member of Bethel Assembly
of God in Juneau, likes to tell how Mr. Personeus invited him to join him
in conducting an Easter sunrise service at the small boat harbor for several
years. Elmer would play Easter hymns on his trombone, then Mr.
Personeus would "preach his heart out" to the boats and whoever might be
aboard, in spite of loud complaints from some of the boats' occupants.

The Personeuses had only lived in their retirement cottage a few years when the highway department condemned their home so the new highway could go through their property. About that same time, they received word from Mrs. Personeus' relatives that her sister Birdie, who was living alone in the LeFevre sisters' house in Lancaster, Pennsylvania, could no longer take care of herself. (Under the pen name "Zenobia Bird," this sister had authored nine Christian novels and had served as associate editor of the *Sunday School Times* for many years.) The relatives thought an excellent solution would be for the Personeuses to come home to the comfortable house left to the LeFevre girls by their aunt, and Birdie would not be alone. Feeling they were needed in Pennsylvania, the Personeuses drove back East to spend the winter. It soon became apparent that Birdie needed more nursing care than the Personeuses could provide. They also felt their work in Alaska was not yet completed, so the house was sold, Birdie was settled into a retirement home, and the Personeuses returned to Alaska. They arrived just in time for the graduation of their granddaughters, AnnaLee Cousart and Barbara Capjohn, the Cousarts' foster daughter, from Seward High School in May 1963.

Barbara Capjohn was born in the Aleut village of Old Harbor on the shore of Kodiak Island. As a very young child, she had contracted a severe case of tuberculosis of the spine and had spent most of her early life in sanitariums, where she had two spinal fusions. Before returning to her home in Old Harbor at the age of nine, she and her older brother, Ralph, also a victim of tuberculosis, were placed for a few months in the Bethel Beach Children's Home, while the Cousarts were in charge. The two children were totally ignorant of the Bible. Knowing their time with them would be short, AnnaMae spent two hours each morning sharing with all the children the story of the Bible. They all sat spellbound. Barbie and Ralph both gave their lives to Jesus. When they tearfully boarded the plane for Old Harbor, the Cousarts gave them each a Bible. Their father, however, forbade them to visit the lady missionary who encouraged them in their walk with the Lord. Instead, he forced them to attend the Russian Orthodox Church with their family. But Barbie often sneaked over to the missionary's house. One time, her father, a fisherman, came home while she was visiting the missionary. Afraid he might beat her, Barbie did not go home. Instead, she spent the night walking the beach. Soon, this became a frequent occurrence. The Aleuts' diet consisted primarily of fish and game, with wild berries added in the late summer. Without fresh fruit and vegetables, Barbie's immune system was weakened. The nights of exposure to the cold, raw winds that swept that treeless island took their toll. The telltale cough that would not go away soon developed into a full-blown case of tuberculosis of the lungs. By the time she was sent to the Mt. Edgecombe Sanitarium near Sitka, her lungs were almost entirely eaten away. The doctors gave her no hope of recovery. When the Cousarts learned of her condition, they immediately wrote letters to Christians across the country, asking them to pray for Barbie's complete healing. Since the doctors believed her case was hopeless, they decided to use her as a human guinea pig for a brand new drug, streptomycin. The results were miraculous. In less than a year, the Alaska Native Service asked the Cousarts if they would take Barbie into their home indefinitely. She would not live to grow up if she were sent back to Old Harbor, they said. The Cousarts were thrilled, but well-meaning friends warned that their three children would be exposed to tuberculosis. Knowing it was God's will, the Cousarts, who no longer operated the children's home, agreed to take her as their foster daughter. And none of their children have ever even tested positive on their tuberculin tests. Barbie, then in fourth grade, lived with the Cousarts until she graduated from high school.

Since the Personeuses no longer had a home in Juneau, they decided to buy one in Seward, a small community south of Anchorage on the Kenai Peninsula, so they could be near the Cousarts. They found property that had two houses, which were old and had been boarded up. The yard was badly overgrown. The location on the main road into town was good, however, and the price within their means, so they bought it for $6,000.00 cash from the $10,000.00 they had been given for their tiny house in Juneau. Though they were in their mid-seventies, they set about fixing the old place. In no time, they had the main house looking cozy and inviting. They painted the outside a cheery yellow with white trim. Grandma pulled out all the weeds by hand and then planted rosebushes and flowers. Later, they even added a small vegetable garden, though the glacial soil required much coaxing to produce her roses and vegetables. Twenty years later, the Personeuses sold this property for nearly seven times what they had paid for it.

The thriving town of Seward spread neatly at the foot of Mt. Marathon, with scenic Resurrection Bay as its eastern and southern boundary. The streets formed a north-south, east-west pattern with the industrial area along the waterfront and the residences nearer the mountains. Resurrection Bay, named by the Russians who first sailed up the bay on Easter Sunday, had long been the main source of income to the city. The natural harbor served as a safe, all-year mooring for ships of all sizes. For this reason, Seward served most of interior Alaska as the gateway for the Alaska Steamship Company, which connected with the 470-mile-long Alaska Railroad to carry supplies to the Interior.

The harbor was also the home base of many fishing vessels. The salmon, halibut, shrimp, and crab, which abound in these coastal waters, were processed in the canneries located on the Seward waterfront. The smell of fish and the clanging of machinery were common along the docks during the summer. Another economic booster was the scenic beauty of Resurrection Bay. Winding through the Chugach Mountains from Anchorage to Resurrection Bay, the Seward Highway offered opportunities to sight moose, mountain sheep, mountain goats, and bears, as well as grand vistas. The annual Fourth of July race up and back down 3,022-foot Mt. Marathon and the annual Silver Salmon Derby, the Army and Air Force recreation camps, and the small fresh water streams teeming with fish attracted tourists, campers, hunters, hikers, and sports fishermen. The community had been selected to receive an All America Cities Award for industry and civic improvement. Resurrection Bay had long been a friend to Seward until a fateful day in March 1964.

Good Friday, March 27, 1964, dawned sunny with a promise of spring. The combined church choirs of Seward were prepared to sing a cantata, *The Seven Last Words* by DuBois, at the Methodist church that evening. Bob and AnnaMae Cousart and their youngest daughter, Kathy, were singing in the cantata, so the Personeuses planned to attend. About 5:30 that evening, AnnaMae and her son Bob (as Robert Paul now liked to be called) dropped by the Personeuses' home to borrow a lace collar AnnaMae wanted to wear that evening.

Entering the glass-enclosed front porch, AnnaMae complimented her mother on the beautiful plants blooming there. After visiting a few minutes, Grandma went to get the collar.

Suddenly, the house began to shake. Thinking her husband was wrestling with his grandson, Grandma staggered out of the bedroom, calling, "What are you doing?"

At that moment, the heavy antique dresser she had been looking in crashed to the floor, slamming the bedroom door behind her. Straight ahead in the kitchen she saw the china closet doors swing open. The fragile antique dishes she had inherited from her mother, many of them over 200 years old, flew out and shattered on the kitchen floor. Helpless to do a thing, she clung to the doorframe, which was shaking so violently she was sure it too would collapse and bring the roof down on top of them all.

AnnaMae clutched the doorframe to the front porch, helplessly watching her mother's beautiful plants topple to the floor one on top of the other.

After five minutes that seemed an eternity, the violent shaking began to subside. Grandpa and AnnaMae hurried to the kitchen to find Grandma standing ankle deep in broken dishes and groceries, shocked and bewildered.

Turning to AnnaMae, Grandpa said, "I wonder what your house looks like!"

"Oh, my!" she gasped. "And Bob's been sick for several days. I wonder how he's doing. Come, Son, we've got to get home!"

They staggered out the door onto the still heaving ground to their car. They were just ready to get in when AnnaMae glanced up and saw a wall of flames about 100 feet high sweeping down the waterfront toward the Texaco oil storage tanks, which were about a block and a half from the Personeuses' home.

AnnaMae ran back to the house, yelling, "Get out of town fast! Those tanks are going to blow!"

The Personeuses grabbed a few things and ran to their car. As they climbed in, two neighbor children dashed up to them. "Please take us with you," they begged. "Our mother hasn't come home from work yet. We're scared!"

"Come along then," Grandma said. They all scrambled into the car and drove away.

The road out of town was crisscrossed with jagged cracks and jumbled debris. The driver of an oncoming car hailed them.

The mother of three of their Sunday school children asked, "Would you please take my children with you? I'm a nurse, and I'm needed at the hospital."

So three more frightened, sobbing children climbed in. Grandma, in her sweet way, quieted the children and prayed for them, their safety, and that of their parents.

As they drove, they had to carefully navigate around burning debris, shattered boats, splintered docks, and fragments of houses. They learned later that a massive slippage in the earth's crust below Prince William Sound in the Gulf of Alaska had generated the most devastating earthquake, known as the Good Friday Earthquake, ever to hit North America, registering a magnitude of 9.2, a force equal to 12,000 Hiroshima-size atomic explosions. When the earthquake hit, the bottom of Resurrection Bay opened up and then closed with such force that it catapulted angry waves into the town. The breakwater, the small boat harbor, the canneries, the docks, and many railroad cars dropped out of sight into the bay. The huge Standard Oil storage tanks ruptured immediately, belching burning oil hundreds of feet into the air. The burning oil raced down the railroad tracks leaving a blazing inferno behind. Within minutes a tidal wave, a *tsunami*, rushed up the bay with such force that it hurled huge railroad cars and engines like sticks and snapped trees like toothpicks. It carried boats and homes several miles before smashing them against cliffs.

Meanwhile, AnnaMae and her son, drove back across town, within a block or so of the burning oil tanks, to the church, with its parsonage attached, to pick up her husband. The floors were covered with debris, but Bob was not there. He had run down the street to help a neighbor. Seeing the car, he dashed back.

Pausing a moment before leaving the house to pick up Kathy at her friend's house, AnnaMae prayed, "Lord, protect Your House and my folks' house too!"

The only way out of town was a two-lane road across the lagoon, bordered by the railroad tracks on one side and cliffs on the other. The Cousarts had driven about two-thirds of the way across the debris-strewn road when the line of cars suddenly slowed. Glancing out the right side of the car, AnnaMae noticed fishing boats, flaming timber, burning oil, and other debris being pushed up and over the railroad tracks, as though by a giant hand.

"Hurry!" she cried. "A tidal wave is coming!"

Just then the line of traffic stopped.

Since no traffic was coming from the opposite direction, Bob pulled out into that lane to pass the line of automobiles. They reached a little knoll at the far side of the lagoon road just as the *tsunami* roared across the highway behind them, smashing houses, boats, and other debris against the cliffs. The water swirled around their tires, but they were high enough to avoid the brunt of the wave. They glimpsed several cars with passengers behind them caught up in the wave, tumbled like toys, and swept toward the cliffs. The fiery debris on the crest of the wave was carried far into the forest at the head of the bay, setting it on fire.

Further down the highway the high school principal hailed the Cousarts. "The bridges are out!" he shouted. "You're welcome to come to my house in Forest Acres."

The roadbed of the highway to Anchorage had sunk six to eight feet lower than the bridges. A series of three of those bridges provided the only way out of the area set afire by the *tsunami*. It looked as though they would be trapped in the burning forest. Then God intervened. The succeeding *tsunami* extinguished the fire!

At the entrance to Forest Acres, a housing development on the outskirts of Seward, the Cousarts met up with the Personeuses. Darkness had descended on the stricken community, although fires and explosions lit the sky all night as the Texaco oil tanks, like erupting volcanoes, blew their tops. The family spent the long, harrowing night with about forty other people in the home of the high school principal with no lights and no heat. Though the calendar said it was spring, the Alaskan night was wintry cold. The Cousarts and the Personeuses were thankful to be together. Many spent that long night not knowing if other family members were alive.

About noon the next day, the weary survivors were allowed to return to their devastated city. Many found only piles of rubble or empty lots where their homes had once stood. The streets were full of shattered houses, smashed boats and cars, upended railroad cars, and railroad ties and piling from the docks stacked up like a giant game of "pickup sticks." The huge oil storage tanks continued to explode for several days. Soot and ashes blackened the town. Numerous aftershocks further terrorized the residents.

When the Personeuses returned to their home, they discovered their neighbors' houses had been extensively damaged by the seismic sea waves. Debris dropped by the waves surrounded the Personeuses' houses within a couple of inches, but no water had entered their houses even though their property was slightly lower than their neighbors'. God had miraculously spared their home. Aside from the broken antique dishes, the only damage was to their chimney and the underpinnings of the floor, which was easily repaired. The church and parsonage also survived with minor damage, although several church families had lost their homes. For several weeks, however, they were without power, water, or sewer.

When the rubble was cleared away from the waterfront area, nothing was left. Ninety-five percent of the industrial area had been destroyed. The canneries, the docks, the boat harbor, and the railroad yards had vanished. In addition, 84 homes in a town with a population of 1,800 had been ruined. Thirty lives had been lost. Twelve bridges along the Seward Highway had collapsed. The land had sunk approximately eight feet, which allowed the tide to wash out huge sections of the railroad and highway. Thus, the tourist trade was cut off, the ships could not dock, and there was no place to process fish. The economic devastation could not have been more complete. But the hardy Alaskans vowed to rebuild.

No public meetings were allowed to be held on Easter Sunday morning, but the survivors gathered for an open air community thanksgiving service on the following Sunday. As president of the Seward Ministerial Association, Bob Cousart preached. Later, in their own service at the Assembly of God, the altars were lined with children, young people, and adults seeking the Lord for salvation.

Grandma recorded her account of the earthquake in poetry:

THE EARTHQUAKE AT SEWARD
Good Friday, March 27, 1964

The day was fair, and all was calm,
The people hurried here and there,
Some thought of pleasure and of fun,
Forgetting God's great Gift, so rare.
Some, in reverence, thought of the day,
Remembered the Lord was crucified,
That the debt of sin He could pay.
When sky grew dark and rocks were rent
As earth did quake when Jesus died that day,
There upon lonely Calvary's hill.

But many failed to think or care,
On this Good Friday, calm and still.

A hush, and then the earth began to tremble,
A convulsive rumble split heaving ground,
Houses rocked, with chimneys falling,
And fissures opened—appalling sound,
Consternation upon all faces;
Shocked, bewildered! Where could one go?
What would happen next? All wondered;
A frantic people rushed to and fro.

Look! Vast pillars of black smoke and fire,
Rising where huge oil tanks had stood,
The flames and smoke are rising higher,
Grim fears swept the whole neighborhood.
Explosions followed, in their turn,
Causing horror, fright, and pity.
It seemed like the whole town would burn,
And people fled, to leave the city,
At least, all those who could.

Cars hastened out upon the highway,
There, to find the bridges gone;
Big cracks and fissures in all directions,
Called a halt until another dawn.
Another horror then confronts us—
A tidal wave, so vast and strong,
Is sweeping onward on the city,
Carrying everything along:
Boats and houses, trains and trailers,
Cars, and logs, things old and new,
Rise on mighty waves of ocean,
Then crashing, vanish from our view.
Canneries, docks, warehouses tumble,
Sinking, as they break in two,
Engulfed, as heaving waters rumble,
Or tossed aside, all bent askew.

165

Night shadows fall, so dark and cold,
Families scattered, gripped with fear,
No lights, no water, we are told.
Huddled in cars, parked far and near,
Or sheltered in some home near town,
We shivered and waited the morning light.
Till day lit up the mountain's crown,
And then, we could see the awful sight.

We gasp. What terrible devastation!
Wrought within so short a time.
Just see the ruin and desolation!
Everything covered with soot and grime.
Glad reunions echoed from so many,
We marvel that so few were missing
Amid that awful holocaust,
Who had thought loved ones were lost.
Amid the ruins, much was standing,
The churches and the schools were spared,
The airport, where planes soon were landing,
All proved God for His people cared.

Then Easter came, so bright and sunny,
Stirring hearts with faith and hope;
Thankful for the homes remaining,
For health and strength with work to cope.
Thankful for God's love and mercy,
Thankful for all good received,
Thankful for kind friends, who helped us,
And our wants and needs relieved.
Seward rallied from the earthquake,
And gathered to give thanks to God,
Faced the trials of the future,
While we walk this earthly sod.

—Florence L. Personeus

CHAPTER 24

A BLUE ROBE

"I have been young, and now am old; yet I have not seen the righteous forsaken, nor his descendants begging bread" (Psalm 37:25). "O God, You have taught me from my youth; and to this day I declare Your wondrous works. Now also when I am old and gray-headed, O God, do not forsake me, until I declare Your strength to this generation, Your power to everyone who is to come" (Psalm 71:17, 18).

For the next 18 years, the Personeuses amazed Alaskans with their hardiness. Into their nineties they were still driving all over their vast state to fill in for pastors. Known affectionately as "Grandma and Grandpa" to everyone, they were a source of inspiration, spiritual encouragement, and stability in an ever-changing Alaskan scene.

God was their Helper and their Healer. When they were sick or in pain, they would pray and praise the Lord. Grandma often told young ladies, "It's better to marry a man of prayer, who can pray the 'effectual fervent prayer of a righteous man' that 'avails much' than to marry a millionaire." When they had a need, they claimed Philippians 4:19, the verse God had given them the day they disembarked for the first time in Juneau in 1917: "And my God shall supply all your need according to His riches in glory by Christ Jesus." Their testimony everywhere they went was Psalm 37:25, "I have been young, and now am old; yet I have not seen the righteous forsaken, nor his descendants begging bread."

The Good Friday Earthquake, which did so much damage to Seward, left every coastal city, town, and connecting highway within a 500-mile arc in similar straits. Several entire villages had been swept into the Gulf of Alaska by the gigantic *tsunami* generated by the quake. More than 100 people had been killed. Thousands had lost their homes. Thousands more were left without heat in freezing temperatures, with smashed dishes, shattered windows, broken water, fuel, and sewer lines. Telephone and electric lines were down. Fires burned out of control.

Anchorage, Alaska's largest city, was one of the hardest hit areas, yet in July First Assembly of God in Anchorage hosted the biennial convention of the Alaskan Assemblies of God. At the previous convention a motion had been adopted that the convention "go on record as favoring the establishing of Alaska as a district and that the Alaska presbyters be requested to draft a proper constitution and bylaws." Assemblies of God churches in Alaska were currently under the administration of the National Home Missions Department, but with statehood, many of the pastors favored the establishment of an Alaska district. Others strongly opposed the proposal. At that time, many of the pastors in Alaska held home missions appointments and thus were eligible to receive pledged support. If Alaska became a district, many of them would lose their national home missions appointments, even though the majority of the churches were not self-supporting at that time. This would cause a financial hardship on these pastors and their families.

This matter dominated the business sessions of the 1964 convention, with much time spent in discussing the pros and cons. Finally, someone called for the vote. Brother Personeus, the "elder statesman" at the convention, had been silent throughout the debate. Suddenly, he leaped to his feet and under the power of the Holy Spirit uttered a message of prophecy, paraphrasing Joshua's charge to the Children of Israel, encouraging the delegates to "be not afraid" but to go forward and "possess the land." When the results of the vote by secret ballot were announced, the required two-thirds majority authorizing the incorporation of the Alaska District had been met. Officers were then elected. The Reverend B. P. Wilson was elected the first District Superintendent and the Personeuses' son-in-law, Robert E. Cousart, the first District Secretary-Treasurer.

Another town particularly hard hit by the earthquake was Valdez, nestled among rugged, glacier-filled mountains on a fjord of Prince William Sound, which was the epicenter of the quake. The waterfront there had vanished completely during the quake. Thirty-one longshoremen had gone to watery graves as the bay swallowed up the dock where they had been unloading a ship. Included in this number was the pastor of the Assemblies of God church in Valdez, Duane Carriker. His wife, Bonnie, bravely carried on the work for a while, but soon found the task overwhelming, so the Personeuses were asked to fill in until a new pastor could be found.

Valdez is noted for its annual snowfall. Thompson Pass, just above Valdez, boasted the second highest annual snowfall in the world, second only to the Himalayas. This was of no concern to Grandpa, who could still shovel snow faster than most men half his age. That winter, however, after a particularly heavy snowfall and a hard day of shoveling snow, Grandpa had what was probably a heart attack, and nearly died. During the attack he saw a vision of heaven. He was thrilled to see all his friends and loved ones who had gone on before, dressed in beautiful white robes, waiting to meet him. Then Jesus held out a blue robe to him. For days afterwards Grandpa grieved over that, wondering why he had not been worthy to receive a white robe, until he finally realized the blue robe was a work robe. God still had more work for him to do on earth before He would call him to his eternal reward. The Lord healed him, and Grandpa never again had trouble with his heart, even though he continued to shovel snow and do other manual labor until he was well over ninety. In fact, he amazed everyone by going swimming in cold Alaskan lakes every summer and ice-skating on frozen ponds each winter until he was 87.

Edgar McElhannon, Alaska District Youth Director in 1965, wanted the youth of the District to honor the Personeuses for their many years of ministry in Alaska. He organized a "This-Is-Your-Life" program, held at First Assembly of God in Anchorage in April 1965. He asked AnnaMae Cousart to compile the Personeuses' life story in slides and narration to be featured in the program. Brother McElhannon invited Brother Personeus to speak at the youth rally. When the Personeuses arrived, however, they were seated on the platform, from which they viewed the portrayal of their life story. At the point in their story where Byron brought home his bride, the slide presentation was paused, the lights came on, and Byron and Marjory, who had been flown in from British Columbia by the Assemblies of God youth of Alaska, entered to surprise the Personeuses. Later in the program, granddaughter AnnaLee, who had come from Fairbanks, where she was attending the University of Alaska, sang the Personeuses' favorite hymn, "Great Is Thy Faithfulness." With their entire family present, the Personeuses rejoiced in the first family reunion since Byron and Marjory had left Alaska for the boat ministry on Vancouver Island about five years earlier.

In June, the Personeuses drove up the Richardson Highway from Valdez to Fairbanks to visit their granddaughter, AnnaLee, who was working there that summer. (She had received a Ford Foundation Earthquake-Related Scholarship that covered all her college expenses for her remaining three years of college since both she and her father had lost employment due to the Good Friday Earthquake. That was a wonderful provision from the Lord since the earthquake had destroyed any means by which she could earn sufficient funds.) The Personeuses stayed with their friend, Agnes Rodli, a missionary to the Arctic who was filling in for the pastor at North Pole, just south of Fairbanks. Going into the house one evening, Grandma stepped back into the open doorway leading to the basement and fell backwards, head first, down a flight of twelve concrete stairs to the concrete basement floor. Fearing she must be dead after such a fall, Grandpa rushed down the stairs after her. Finding her alive, he began to pray for her. Amazingly, she had broken no bones, although she was bruised and shaken, and soon she was able to walk up the stairs.

The next Sunday morning back in Valdez, where they were still interim pastors, Grandma began blacking out whenever she tried to get out of bed. She still had a large lump on her head from her fall. Afraid she was dying, Grandpa called his daughter in Seward. AnnaMae called the District Superintendent, as well as other pastors around Alaska, asking them to pray for Sister Personeus. After Grandpa laid hands on her in prayer, he had to go into the church, which adjoined the parsonage. When he had gone, the Lord spoke to Grandma in a still, small voice, "You can lie here and be waited on, or get up and be healed." So she got up. Grandpa had just requested prayer for her in Sunday school when she walked in—completely healed.

The next day the Personeuses drove a friend up to sightsee in McKinley National Park, where they happened to meet Brother Wilson, the District Superintendent.

"Sister Personeus," he exclaimed, "you don't look the least bit like a dying woman!"

On April 5, 1966, the Personeuses celebrated their fiftieth wedding anniversary. By this time, a new pastor had come to Valdez, so the Personeuses had moved back to their cozy little home in Seward. AnnaMae made a large wedding cake and held an open house at the parsonage in honor of her parents' anniversary. Grandma wrote this poem as a tribute to Grandpa for their golden wedding anniversary:

THE LORD HATH NEED OF HIM

Mark 11:1-3

'Twas only a colt by the roadside,
But 'twas needed by Jesus our Lord,
"Go, loose the colt," and tell any man,
"The Lord hath need of him," is His word,
"Loose him, and let him go."

A young man toiled in a printing shop,
But he caught the vision of souls—
Lost and undone, without God or His Son,
While time swiftly onward rolls;
He was tied by duties at home.

A widowed mother needed his care.
How could he leave her alone?
Then a brave younger sister took the task.
He was free to leave his own.
She loosed him, and let him go.

He went to Alaska, blazing a trail,
Preaching the Full Gospel up there,
A pioneer in that northern land,
Alaska, so new and so fair,
The Lord had need of him there.

Forty-six years he labored on,
First, in one place, and then another,
'Mid trials, testing, and hardships,
To lift some fallen brother,
The Lord had need of him there.

Then back to the East Coast again they came,
And duties seemed to bind them there.
The Lord provided a pleasant home
Among dear friends, who seemed to care.
Why should he want to go?

A gray-haired man, no longer young,
Was told, "You need to rest."
Six months they stayed, then calmly said,
"Let us go back and do our best,
Loose us, and let us go."

"It is time to rest," they told him.
"At home you can take some ease."
"But Alaska needs more workers,
Let us go back, if you please,
Loose us, and let us go."

Nearly fifty years in the northland cold
They worked in all kinds of weather
To witness and to help wherever told,
Working faithfully together,
The Lord had need of them.

"GO YE," is the message Christ gave us.
GO YE to those who have not heard.
GO YE in the name of Christ Jesus.
GO quickly! Preach God's Holy Word.
The Lord hath need of YOU.

—Florence L. Personeus

By the spring of 1966, the Cousarts felt their work in Seward was completed. They were asked to take the pastorate in Valdez, as that church was again in need of a pastor. After their son, Robert Paul, had graduated from high school in May, they began the arduous task of moving to Valdez.

The church in Valdez was a picturesque, New England-style building with a roomy parsonage attached. The Cousarts soon learned, however, that they would not be allowed to remain in that lovely setting more than a year. The entire town of Valdez had been condemned! After the earthquake, divers of the Coast and Geodetic Survey exploring the coastline below the water level had been thoroughly frightened to discover that Valdez was now perched on a ledge that could break off into the icy blue waters at any time! Instead of solid ground, there was water beneath the town! A new site for the town was found, and the whole town had to be moved five miles west.

The Cousarts asked the Personeuses to come to Valdez to assist with the work in the new town, since Bob had to be away on business as Secretary-Treasurer of the Alaska District from time to time. After renting their two houses and a trip to California to visit Grandpa's younger brother Lyman and to British Columbia to help Byron as he recovered from surgery and hepatitis, the Personeuses arrived in Valdez in the spring of 1967. They were just in time to attend their granddaughter Kathy's graduation from high school in the new town. The new church had been completed, but much work was yet to be done before the Cousarts could move into the new parsonage.

On June 10, 1967, the first wedding in the new town of Valdez was held at the Assembly of God. AnnaLee, who had graduated from the University of Alaska three weeks earlier, married Second Lieutenant Robert J. Conti, also a 1967 graduate of the University of Alaska. Grandpa performed the first part of the ceremony until the father of the bride had given her away; then he stepped back to let her father, Bob Cousart, complete the ceremony.

Bob Conti had come to Alaska in 1959 with his father, a colonel in the United States Air Force, to Eielson Air Force Base near Fairbanks. When he had finished high school, his parents had been transferred, and he had remained in Fairbanks to attend the University. As a child, Bob was not taken to church. When he was eight years old, his father had been stationed in Greece, and the family had accompanied him. Another American wife stationed in Greece had often visited the Conti family. She had frequently lamented the fact that she had not been in church for years.

"God must hate me," she said.

173

Young Bob thought, "I've never even gone to church. God must *really* hate *me*."

Early one Sunday morning while Bob was sitting in a tree near the road just outside of Athens, a unit of Greek soldiers marched by on their way to the Orthodox Church. Lustily, they sang hymns as they marched. Hearing them, eight-year-old Bob felt very guilty because he never went to church. Suddenly, a warm Presence enveloped him, as though God had put His loving arms around him, and he felt God assuring him that He loved him.

The first thing Bob did was to go to the Orthodox Church. The two-dimensional icons frightened him. Then a priest with an upside-down stovepipe hat chased him away. Frightened, Bob decided he would have to wait until they returned to the States to find a church. Bob was eleven when they returned. It was then he learned that as a baby he had been baptized a Catholic. A friend took him to church where a priest enrolled him in special classes to prepare him for confirmation.

Bob faithfully followed the Catholic Church until a priest gave him a *Good News for Modern Man* translation of the New Testament. He loved reading the stories about Jesus, but soon he had many questions. The priest told him to just trust the Church. "The layman cannot understand the Bible," he said. But that didn't satisfy Bob. When he graduated from high school, he left the Catholic Church. Then at the University of Alaska in Fairbanks he met a Christian girl who invited him to church. There, the evangelist spoke on Jesus' words in John 10:9, "I am the door. If anyone enters by Me, he will be saved, and will go in and out and find pasture." That night, Bob walked through that Door.

A year later, he met AnnaLee at an Intervarsity prayer meeting at the University of Alaska. He knew nothing about the baptism in the Holy Spirit, but after two and a half years of courtship, he decided that after they were married, he would go with her to the Assemblies of God church in Fairbanks. Then in September 1967, three months after they were married, he went on active duty with the Army. Enroute to his assignment, he took his new bride home to meet his parents at Hanscom Field, just outside of Boston.

To help out with the church and living expenses, Bob Cousart and Grandpa obtained the contract as custodians of the Valdez post office, which included shoveling snow. Early every morning and at closing time

Grandpa loved to be there, shoveling snow, putting up or taking down the flag, or mopping the lobby. But best of all, he enjoyed greeting all the people.

Grandma put her love of gardening to good use once again by planting a myriad of colorful flowers around the new church and parsonage. She also continued to carry on her large volume of correspondence, sending hundreds of birthday cards and letters a year. Since she loved to write poetry, she often wrote poetic acrostics of people's names in their birthday cards. She was thrilled when Ada Buchwalter Bolton and her sister Mary Lewer, her old friends from Paradise, Pennsylvania, who had introduced her to Pentecost (they had spent many years as missionaries to China), visited her in Valdez.

During these years the Personeuses' family expanded as Byron and Marjory, who had wanted children for years, were finally able to adopt a little girl, Chantal. Then Kathy married Tom McAlpine and Barbara Capjohn, the Cousarts' foster daughter, married Eng Kim "Casey" Chu. In 1970, the Personeuses became great-grandparents when Kathy and AnnaLee both gave birth to baby boys, Eugene Edward McAlpine and Robert Benjamin Conti.

In March 1972, the Cousarts moved to Fairbanks, the location of the Alaska District office, so the Personeuses returned to their home in Seward, where they immediately became active again in that Assembly. Grandpa also served as a local and state advisor for Women's Aglow. In 1973, Peter Castro, who had come to know the Lord in their mission in Juneau in the 1920s and had returned to his native Philippines as a missionary, brought his wife to visit the Personeuses. They accompanied the Personeuses to District Council in Fairbanks in April and were able to greet the many church leaders who had supported his work over the years.

The fall of 1973, Bob Cousart resigned as Secretary-Treasurer of the Alaska District in order to accept a pastorate in Naches, Washington, where their daughter Kathy and her family lived. The Personeuses continued to reside in Seward.

In June 1975, the pastor of the church in Nenana, about 50 miles west of Fairbanks, asked the Personeuses to fill in for them while they went on furlough. Cheerfully leaving their newly planted garden to the weeds, they drove more that 600 miles to Nenana. When they arrived, Grandpa noticed a huge load of mill slabs (the part that is cut off the trees to even them up before they are cut into lumber) had been dumped in the yard for use as firewood. Grandpa told the pastor that he would stack them up for him. Some of the slabs were 15 feet long, and in stacking them Grandpa, who was then 87 years old, had to throw them up over his head. Worried he might hurt himself, Grandma told him to be careful, but he just laughed. In spite of his good physical condition, the strain proved to be too much for him. He tore a muscle in his hip.

He drove back to Anchorage, a trip of about 500 miles, and went to a chiropractor. The treatment aggravated his condition, and he landed in the hospital for 13 days—his first stay in a hospital in his life. Thinking he was too old for them to do much for him, the hospital staff gave him no real treatment. Prior to his injury, he had stood straight and tall; afterwards, he stood crooked for the rest of his life. He left the hospital in a wheelchair, so the Cousarts persuaded the Personeuses to come to Naches to stay with them.

For the next 10 months, the only way Grandpa could get comfortable enough to sleep was to sit in a reclining chair. Soon, he was out of the wheelchair and walking with crutches, and then with a cane. By the spring of 1976, even though he still experienced a lot of pain, he insisted he was ready to go back to Alaska in time for District Council in April.

District Council that year was held in Anchorage. One evening, a special missionary offering was collected which amounted to $25,000.00. Grandpa became so excited he rushed up to the platform exclaiming, "What hath God wrought? I never dreamed anything like that could be possible!"

Then the anointing of the Spirit fell on him, and he danced all around the platform for three or four minutes. He said he felt the power on him for about 15 minutes in all. When the power lifted, he realized he no longer had any pain for the first time since his injury. He was healed! What a time of rejoicing filled the church that night!

About this time, Grandpa decided he wanted to do more for the Lord, so he started a weekly radio program on the local station in Seward. The 15-minute program, which he described as "a message from a senior citizen," consisted of taped Gospel songs followed by a brief message, with an invitation to attend the Seward Assembly of God. When the Personeuses were out of town, Grandpa would make tapes and mail them to the station. He continued his radio programs until he was 97½ years old, when his hearing became too poor to continue. Then, until his death the next year, he continued to pay for a 15-minute broadcast by the pastor of the Seward church.

For many years, Brother Fred Vogler, the first executive officer of the Education and Home Missions Department at the Assemblies of God Headquarters in Springfield, Missouri, had used a prayer schedule for world missions. When he died, Grandpa wrote to Sister Vogler, asking her to send him her husband's prayer schedule. One time when the Personeuses were visiting the Contis in Springfield, the clock struck the hour, and according to Bob Conti, Grandpa jumped up exclaiming, "It's time to pray for Africa!" He headed for the bedroom. Bob heard his knees hit the floor as he began to intercede for the missionaries and lost souls.

Grandpa was always concerned with "passing the torch" of ministry. One of his biggest thrills was to participate in the ordination of his grandson-in-law, Robert J. Conti, in the New York District in May 1979. Bob had planned to make the military a career, but while he was in Vietnam, he had come to an understanding of the universal nature of sin. As an infantry battalion intelligence officer, his job had included searching the bodies of enemy soldiers killed in battle to determine from their personal effects where they had come from. On one body Bob found a notebook full of detailed drawings of the human anatomy and a letter. The battalion surgeon said it appeared he had wanted to be an obstetrician. The battalion interpreter determined the letter was addressed to the young man's fiancée. He had written of his desire to get married after the war and go to Paris to study medicine. But he was dead. And the intelligence information Bob had gathered had led to this man's death. Neither had wanted to kill anyone. But due to the universal nature of sin, a young man who only wanted to bring life into the world was now dead. Until then, Bob had thought of sin in terms of what one did personally, such as breaking the Ten Commandments. He had believed that being an Army officer and ridding the world of Communists was the best thing he could do to bring peace to this world. In Vietnam he had begun to realize that sin, not Communism, was the real enemy. Two years later, he had resigned his regular Army commission to study for the ministry. In 1973, he and AnnaLee had moved to Springfield, Missouri, so he could attend Central Bible College and then the Assemblies of God Theological

Seminary, where he had earned a Bachelor of Arts in Bible and a Master of Divinity.

In May 1977, the Contis had moved to New York to start a new church planting in Gloversville. The Personeuses observed that the Contis had gone to New York exactly 60 years from the time they had left New York to go to Alaska in 1917. Two years later, Bob was approved for ordination. As the brethren, including Brother Personeus and Brother Cousart, laid hands on Bob to pray the ordination prayer, the Holy Spirit fell on Grandpa, and he uttered a message in tongues and interpretation.

Following the New York District Council, the Personeuses, accompanied by the Cousarts, visited in Gloversville, then continued on to Connecticut and Pennsylvania to visit relatives. This trip proved to be the Personeuses' last trip East. They were 91 years old.

Upon arriving back in Alaska, the Personeuses invited the Cousarts to visit them. They wanted to visit all the churches they could drive to in Alaska, but Grandpa did not feel he should do all that driving himself. For two wonderful weeks, the Cousarts drove them all over the state, finally taking the ferry from Haines to Juneau. The Cousarts flew home from there, but the Personeuses visited Pelican for the last time. The little trees they had planted near the church had grown tall, and the little children they had ministered to had become men and women—some of them serving the Lord. The little church on the hill still stood as a Gospel lighthouse to the fishermen and cannery workers who sailed or flew up Lizianski Inlet.

CHAPTER 25

THE END OF THE TRAIL

"I have fought the good fight, I have finished the race, I have kept the faith. Finally, there is laid up for me the crown of righteousness, which the Lord, the righteous Judge, will give to me on that Day, and not to me only but also to all who have loved His appearing" (2 Timothy 4:7, 8).
"Precious in the sight of the Lord is the death of His saints"
(Psalm 116:15).

New Year's Day, 1980, dawned clear and very cold in Seward. Snow had drifted against the Personeuses' house and frozen around the door. Grandpa had been able to open the door a little ways but then could not shut it again. They had hung a quilt over the door to try to keep out the cold, but even wearing extra clothing, Grandma could hardly keep warm as the cold wind rattled the windows. As she bustled from the living room to the little kitchen, she suddenly turned her ankle and found herself on the floor in an awkward position. Grandpa could not get her up, and she was in great pain. He quickly phoned their pastor, Larry Schlak, who came immediately to pray for her. When he could not get her up, he called the ambulance. The pastor and the ambulance attendants had to chop their way through the ice to get the door opened wide enough for the stretcher.

At the Seward Hospital X-rays were taken, which showed that Grandma had broken her hip and bones in her hand. Since she would need surgery to put a pin in her hip, it was necessary to transport her by ambulance to a larger hospital in Anchorage, 130 miles of winding highway north of Seward. The weather was so cold that the ambulance she was riding in froze up at Moose Pass, 28 miles north of Seward, and she had to wait three hours in the unheated vehicle until another ambulance could be driven down from Anchorage. The thermometer outside registered 32 degrees below zero Fahrenheit! She finally arrived in Anchorage at 11:00 o'clock that night. The next day surgery was performed.

The doctor in Seward had put a cast on her broken hand. It went half way up her arm. During the night she dreamed her hand was stuck inside a canning jar in a snow bank, and she had to work hard to wiggle it out. In the morning, the nurses found she had somehow managed to pull her slim hand out of the cast!

During her stay in the Anchorage hospital she overheard a nurse say, "I'm supposed to get that old lady up, but she'll never walk again!"

That challenged Grandma to prove her wrong. Within six weeks she could walk without a walker, although she was supposed to use one to prevent another fall.

Being in the hospital for the first time in her 91 years was hard on Grandma. She was accustomed to helping others. Now, she had to lie back and allow others to take care of her. For a while she became depressed. Her faith was severely tested. She wondered if she had let God down somehow. Perhaps He had allowed her to break her hip as punishment, she thought. Then, the thought plagued her that maybe God had failed her by allowing the accident. After she had been in the hospital for nearly a month, the doctor thought she was well enough to fly to Washington to the Cousarts' home in Kittitas, where she was able to get around quite well in a wheelchair and with the use of the walker. Soon, she was walking with just a cane and before long, without any mechanical help at all. As her mobility returned, and as she spent time with her family, her indomitable spirit was soon restored. By May, she was well enough for them to return to their own home in Seward.

Because the Personeuses were finding it more difficult to deal with the harsh Alaskan winters, they returned to Kittitas in December. Grandma's eyesight had grown steadily worse until she could no longer keep up with her correspondence. Her beautiful, schoolgirl handwriting was just as firm and lovely as ever, but to write a letter required much effort. She had to hold a large magnifying glass in one hand in order to see what she was writing. Eventually, she had to abandon the magnifying glass and use her left hand to mark the place as she wrote by feel.

The day before their sixty-fifth wedding anniversary on April 5, 1981, Grandma tripped on the bedspread in their room in the Cousarts' home and fell, breaking several ribs. She refused to take pills for the pain, but whenever it became unbearable, Grandpa would pray for her until it subsided. Though she was in a lot of pain, she still attended the celebration the next day. More than one hundred friends came from near and far. The Personeuses had not seen some of them for many years.

The Personeuses had wanted to return to Alaska in time for the District Council in April, but Grandma's health would not allow it. Her ribs were healing nicely, but when AnnaMae went in to fix her hair one morning in May, Grandma was experiencing severe pain in her back. She thought it was arthritis aggravated by eating sweets. AnnaMae had to be away for a few days, and when she returned, she was shocked at her mother's appearance. When she took her to the emergency room, they learned that three of her vertebrae had collapsed from osteoporosis. Nothing could be done to help her. When the pain became unbearable, Grandpa would pray. In spite of her pain, she insisted on attending the services at the church.

One Sunday morning, after a particularly painful night, Grandma called Bob into her room. "I want to speak to you as my pastor, not as my son-in-law," she said. "Will I be letting the Lord down if I just lie here in bed this morning? I want to go to church, but it hurts so much just to move."

Bob assured her that God understands our infirmities; then they prayed together that God would give her the wisdom to know what she should do. She decided to stay home that day.

In July, the Cousarts attended a camp meeting near Spokane for two days. The Personeuses wanted to go along. In one of the services God marvelously touched Grandma and took away all the pain from her back. By the end of the month they were back in Alaska!

Byron and Marjory spent their two-week vacation in Seward that summer helping the Personeuses sort through their belongings in preparation for selling their home. Byron also persuaded his father, who at 93 was still driving (and his driver's license was good for two more years) to sell his car. When he had renewed his license at the age of 92, no one had even questioned his age since he looked so young. (He enjoyed asking people who serviced his car or waited on him in a store to guess how old he was. Most of them guessed he was 65!) In October, the Personeuses returned to Kittitas for the winter.

The year 1982 marked the sixty-fifth anniversary of the founding of the first Assemblies of God church in Alaska. The Alaska District wanted to honor the Personeuses at the District Council in April, so they paid their fare to Fairbanks, where the anniversary council was convened. The Cousarts traveled with them to assist them.

Barbara Chu, the Cousarts' foster daughter, flew up from Juneau to meet them in Fairbanks, even though she had not been feeling well for several months. After the District Council, the Personeuses returned to Seward for the summer and fall so they could try to sell their home. In June, they were saddened to learn that Barbie Chu had been diagnosed with inoperable cancer of the pancreas. They visited her in the hospital in Anchorage where she was undergoing radiation treatments. Barbie returned to Juneau in September, and the Personeuses flew south for the winter.

The church the Personeuses had founded in Juneau wanted to celebrate the church's sixty-fifth anniversary during the first week of December, so they invited the Personeuses and Cousarts to be their guests of honor. That week, Bethel Christian Center held a banquet and special services, and the Personeuses and Cousarts greeted many old friends, some who still lived in Juneau and many who had moved away but who had returned for the celebration. The church had moved out to the Mendenhall Valley, about ten miles from downtown Juneau. The congregation had grown rapidly and had added a school for preschool through twelfth grade.

Barbie Chu was so happy to see them once again. But on December 6, Barbie had to be hospitalized. The doctors said she could pass away at any time. Reluctantly, the Personeuses and Cousarts had to say "good-bye" and return to their duties in Kittitas.

Several inches of new snow lay on the ground when they arrived home. They unloaded the car and helped Grandma into the house, but they could not find Grandpa. Finally, they discovered him—he was out shoveling snow!

January 13, Grandpa turned 95. Two days later, they received word that Barbie had gone to be with the Lord. She was only 42 and had left behind a husband and two children, Cassandra and Kenneth. Grandma and Grandpa struggled with questions about Barbie's death. They, along with many others, had prayed for her healing many times. Why had she not been healed? Yet, they knew she had gone to a place where she would never again suffer pain, sickness, or death. And while she was in the hospital, she had been able to speak to many visitors about their souls, and some had committed their lives to Christ. Before she died, Barbie told her pastor, "I have conquered death. I no longer fear it."

In May 1983, the Personeuses' granddaughter, AnnaLee Conti, was ordained to the Full Gospel ministry in New York. Unable to be present, the Personeuses and the Cousarts sent a telegram: "Congratulations on your ordination. May God's richest blessings rest upon your ministry. Wish we could be there to share this happy occasion. Your grandmother, grandfather, great-grandfather, and great-great-grandfather were all ordained in New York State. Love and prayers, Mom and Dad Cousart, Grandma and Grandpa Personeus." This telegram was read aloud in the ordination service. AnnaLee became the fifth generation ordained minister in the Personeus family.

That fall Grandpa became very sick and had to be hospitalized. Tests indicated severe pancreatitis due to gallstones. Because of his advanced age, the doctor put him on a strict fat-free diet rather than risking surgery. What a trial that diet was for him! He especially missed his peanut butter and icing on his cake. Aside from this minor inconvenience, his health remained remarkably good.

Grandma's health, however, began to deteriorate rapidly. When she was about seventy, the scar from the lump the Lord had removed from her breast years earlier in Pelican became a sore that would not heal. Gradually, over a 20-year period, it spread over a large area of her upper body, leaving a painful, open wound. By 1984, she had become quite confused much of the time, except when it was her turn to pray during family devotions. The day before their sixty-eighth wedding anniversary, she again fell and broke several ribs. Even though she could not tolerate any tight binding due to the extent of the cancer, she was up the next day for the celebration of their anniversary.

Then, on July 2, she slipped in the bathroom and fell, breaking her right hip. In spite of her age, the doctors recommended surgery to replace the broken hip with a steel ball. She came through the surgery remarkably well, but because the Cousarts could no longer do all that was needed to adequately care for her at home, she entered the Royal Vista Care Center in Ellensburg. The nursing home was about two blocks from the church Bob Cousart pastored, so every morning on his way to the church Bob would drop Grandpa off to spend the day with Grandma.

In spite of intense pain from the cancer, Grandma remained sweet and gentle, never complaining of any discomfort. She won the hearts of everyone who cared for her. She adamantly refused, however, to take her medications. The nurses had to secretly mix it in her food.

On her birthday, November 3, the Cousarts, with the help of their daughter Kathy, who is a nurse, brought Grandma home for a few hours. Grandpa wanted her to stay home with them. When they kept her overnight at Christmas, however, he realized how impossible it was for them to care for her at home. Once again he struggled with questions. Why did God not heal her of cancer when He had healed her so many times in the past?

The Personeuses celebrated their sixty-ninth (and last) wedding anniversary with cake and punch at the nursing home. One elderly lady, pointing to Grandma, complained to AnnaMae, "She preached to me!"

Even though she was often confused, Grandma was ready always to tell everyone about her Lord. When anyone asked her how she was, she would raise her hand and say, "I'm praising the Lord!"

Bob would sometimes respond, "Mom, I didn't ask you what you are doing! I asked how you are!"

She would laugh and say, "Oh, I hurt some, but praise the Lord anyway!"

As the Cousarts said "good-bye" to Grandma at the end of what proved to be their last visit, Bob said, "We're going to pray for you now, Mom."

"You ought to praise more," she urged sweetly. "We all must praise the Lord more. That's what He wants." Ministering to the Lord and to others had been her life from childhood.

On June 4, 1985, the nurse was preparing to feed Grandma lunch when Jesus called her home. She slumped over in her chair and slipped quietly into the presence of her Lord and Savior at the age of 96½. Although everyone would miss her greatly, her funeral was a joyous celebration of her life and her heavenly coronation, with the singing of "Great Is Thy Faithfulness" and "What a Day That Will Be." She was buried in the cemetery in Ellensburg, Washington.

After 69 years with Grandma, Grandpa was very lonesome without her. The cemetery could be seen from the Cousarts' church. After services Grandpa would stand on the steps and gaze toward the cemetery, often asking to be taken to the gravesite. Grandma had always been the storyteller, but after her death Grandpa often reminisced about the early days, telling stories of his childhood and early ministry his family had never heard him tell before.

Grandpa was always ready to accompany the Cousarts wherever they went. They visited Byron and Marjory, who had retired from the boat ministry. They had moved to Nanoose Bay, British Columbia, where they served as assistant caretakers for the Pentecostal campgrounds there. Grandpa especially enjoyed the ministers' fellowship meetings. One time he accompanied the Cousarts to the Silver Lake Camp Meeting, where Evangelist Lowell Lundstrum was the camp speaker. Grandpa had become quite shaky on his feet, so he often used the wheelchair on longer trips. Brother Lundstrum welcomed Grandpa and had the congregation place a special offering in Grandpa's wheelchair for him to buy the new hearing aids he needed.

On August 29, 1986, Byron, Marjory, and Chantal met the Cousarts, Grandpa, his grandson Bob and his wife Becky with their three girls, and Kathy with her two children at Lake Chelan for a family picnic to celebrate Byron's birthday. Grandpa watched Byron and Bob play a game of lawn darts. After a while, Grandpa tottered out of his lawn chair and with a playful grin, joined their game. He really seemed to enjoy himself that day.

On Monday, October 6, Grandpa accompanied the Cousarts to a fellowship meeting in Yakima. He testified in his own electrifying way in a strong voice, causing the whole congregation to respond with resounding praises. Everyone complimented him on how well he looked. At 98½, he looked like he could easily make his one-hundredth birthday.

Tuesday and Wednesday, the Cousarts attended a ministers and spouses retreat in Yakima, an hour's drive away. AnnaMae fixed Grandpa's lunch and dinner before they left each day. Tuesday evening Grandpa complained of an earache and asked AnnaMae for the eardrops his doctor had given him for impacted wax. The next morning when they went to say "good-bye," he asked for more eardrops. Late that evening, when the Cousarts arrived home, they discovered that Grandpa had not eaten his lunch or dinner and had not been out of bed all day. He seemed "out of it." When he had to go to the bathroom, he couldn't get out of bed, so Bob had to help him. They put him in his recliner and tried to make him comfortable, but about 4:00 o'clock in the morning, AnnaMae realized he was delirious and called an ambulance to take him to the hospital.

After doing some tests, the doctor told AnnaMae that her father had an ear infection that had gone into meningitis. He was so sick, the doctor told her, that he would probably die. If he lived, he would probably be in a vegetative state. The high fever caused him to suffer repeated grand mal seizures. Every so often he would stop breathing, then suddenly start breathing again. Friday evening, he quieted. Then at 7:40 in the evening, with his granddaughter Kathy holding his hand, he slipped from this life into the presence of the Lord he had served so faithfully for 83 years. He had finally received his white robe.

At that very moment, the Personeuses' 16-year-old grandson, Robert Benjamin Conti, in Huntington Station, New York, was telling his visiting Aunt Audrey and Uncle Jack Cousart of his intention to enter Bible college to study for the ministry in answer to God's call on his life. The torch had passed to a new generation. (Bob B. Conti completed pastoral studies at Valley Forge Christian College in Phoenixville, Pennsylvania, and served as an assistant pastor for several years. He then completed courses for obtaining a teaching certificate and is teaching first grade in the public schools in Newburgh, New York, and is doing children's ministries in his church. The Personeuses' grandson, Robert Paul "Bob" Cousart, and granddaughter, Kathy McAlpine, are both active in their churches. Granddaughter Chantal Personeus Thomas has opened her home to many foster children. And their grandson-in-law, Bob Conti, in addition to pastoring, is involved in a radio ministry. The Personeuses' ministry continues through their descendants.)

The funeral director later told AnnaMae he had been shocked when he had received the call to go to the hospital to pick up Mr. Personeus' body. "I had just seen him on Monday, and he was fine," he said. "I told my two young assistants to look at a man who was almost 100 years old, yet he didn't even look 65. I told them, 'That shows you what living a good, clean life can do for you.'"

The Assembly of God in Ellensburg was filled as friends and loved ones gathered from near and far to bid farewell. AnnaLee Conti and her son Bob flew in from New York, and she sang several of Grandpa's favorite songs at the funeral. Edward L. Hughes, Assistant Superintendent of the Alaska District, who had grown up in the Juneau Children's Home, represented all the Alaskan churches at the funeral. Other guest pastors who shared in the service included Clifford L. Hobson, Secretary-Treasurer of the Northwest District; Thomas Rideout, Presbyter of the

Yakima Section; and R. J. Carlson, former Superintendent of the Northwest District. Bob Cousart officiated. Grandpa was buried beside Grandma, but his loved ones know that they are together again in Glory, praising the Lord they served together so many years.

The Superintendent of the Alaska District, Wesley J. Bransford, wrote in *The Alaska Missionary:* "A great Alaskan pioneer has now joined his wife in heaven...The Personeus family has given us a legacy of what pioneering churches is all about. We of the Alaska District owe a debt of gratitude for the solid heritage bequeathed to us through the long and faithful ministry of the Personeuses. Their example is an inspiration, and we are indeed grateful for their sterling example of faith and perseverance over these many years...May we all be faithful to glorify God in everything we do, as were Reverend and Mrs. C. C. Personeus."

The Personeuses never pastored a large church. Yet, they touched the lives of hundreds, maybe thousands, because they were willing to overlook their disappointments and faithfully exercise their ministry gifts of evangelism and hospitality. God had placed them in crucial locations where they came in contact with many transients—in Juneau with the miners and fishermen, in Ketchikan with the servicemen of World War II, in Pelican with the seasonal fishermen and cannery workers. The Personeuses brought these lonely people into their home, demonstrated the love of Christ to them, won many of them to the Lord, and discipled them as quickly as possible. As they returned to their homes, these converts took the salvation message with them. Thus, the ministry of the Personeuses affected not only the future of the Alaskan churches they pioneered, but the Pentecostal message spread out in ever-increasing waves in the United States and around the world as many of their converts caught their missionary vision as well.

The Personeuses have explored and conquered their frontiers of faith. They have found their Heavenly City. They have left us an example to follow. Now, it is up to us to face the challenge of exploring and conquering the frontiers of our faith, so that we too may hear from our Savior, "Well done, good and faithful servant."

Perhaps you have been challenged to begin exploring the frontiers of your faith, but you have never accepted Christ as your personal Lord and Savior. That is the first step. And it is so simple even a child can understand how. **First**, you must admit you are a sinner. Romans 3:23 says, "For all have sinned and fall short of the glory of God." **Second**, you must believe that Jesus' death on the Cross paid the penalty for *your* sins. Acts 16:31 says, "Believe on the Lord Jesus Christ, and you will be saved." **Third**, You must confess your sins to Jesus and ask Him to forgive you and help you to live a life pleasing to Him. First John 1:9 says, "If we confess our sins, He is faithful and just to forgive us our sins and to cleanse us from all unrighteousness." You are now a child of God. John 1:12 promises, "But as many as received Him, to them He gave the right to become children of God, even to those who believe in His name." In order to grow in your new life, you need to read the Bible and pray every day and find a Bible-believing church where you can fellowship regularly with other Christians. Acts 2:42 says, "And they continued steadfastly in the apostles' doctrine and fellowship, in the breaking of bread, and in prayers." May God bless you as you begin your new life in Christ exploring your own frontiers of faith.

Carl and Florence Personeus c. 1958.

Revisiting the Haines to Klukwan road. Mrs. Personeus stands in front of 'glaciered' cliff along the side of the road.

**Mr. Personeus inside the Tlingit tribal house in Klukwan
with his interpreter and Anna Katzeek.**

The Personeuses in Tlingit tribal dress (1938).

Klukwan people who had been children and young people in congregation in 1922-23.

**Personeuses with their former interpreter
(to r. of Mr. Personeus) and other Klukwan converts.**

**Personeus Family reunion at the "This is Your Life"
Program in 1965.**

**(back row l. to r.: Byron and Marjory Personeus, Robert Paul
Cousart, AnnaMae Personeus Cousart and Robert E. Cousart; front
row l. to r.: Kathy Cousart, Florence and Carl Personeus, Barbara
Capjohn, AnnaLee Cousart)**

Going to church in Valdez—the new town.

**Carl Personeus shoveling snow at the parsonage in
Valdez at age 82 in 1970.**

The Peter Castros from the Philippines visit the Personeuses in Seward in 1973. Peter was saved in the early days of the Personeuses' ministry in Juneau and returned to his country as a missionary.

Family reunion at the Personeuses' sixtieth wedding anniversary celebration.

(front row l. to r.: Robert Benjamin Conti, Chantal Personeus, Kenneth and Cassandra Chu, Eugene McAlpine; 2nd row: Barbara Capjohn Chu, Carl and Florence Personeus, Kathy Cousart McAlpine holding Cherie McAlpine; 3rd row: AnnaLee Cousart Conti, AnnaMae Personeus Cousart, Marjory Personeus, Tom McAlpine; 4th row: Robert J. Conti, Robert E. Cousart, Byron Personeus)

Fourth of July parade float in Seward featured the Personeuses.

The Personeuses at District Council at Barrow, Alaska.

MORE POEMS BY
FLORENCE L. PERSONEUS

MY OLD ALASKA HOME

(To the tune of "My Old Kentucky Home")

The sun shines bright
In my old Alaska home,
'Tis summer, the young folks are gay,
But my heart feels sad,
For I think of those who roam,
All the dear ones, now so far away.

Refrain:
Though we may be parted
From those we love so dear,
We can still rejoice,
There's a better Home above,
With our Lord, and
No partings there to fear.

Oh, those happy days
We spent in Ketchikan,
Along with the clouds and the rain,
For the Heavenly Sunshine
Brightened every plan,
And soon the sun would shine again.

Now that happy group
Is scattered far and wide,
To the east and the west
Some have gone,
And some to the north,
And others to the south,
While a few still help to carry on.

There were days of toil,
Then evening brought release,
And we gathered in fellowship sweet,
While in our hearts
We felt God's joy and peace,
As around His Word we'd gladly meet.

But those days are gone,
And many loved ones now
Are far from our dim, wistful sight,
So we breathe a prayer,
God bless and keep them true,
Then my old Alaska home, good night.

—Florence L. Personeus

(Written for the servicemen in Ketchikan, Alaska, during World War II.)

LOOK UP!

(Based on Titus 2:13)

Swiftly the days are coming and going,
On towards the oceans, the rivers are flowing,
Some days of sunshine, others 'tis snowing,
And Jesus has told us: "LOOK UP!"

Over the world jet bombers are flying,
Hearts fail with fear and many are dying,
People rush on, though weary and sighing,
But Jesus has told us: "LOOK UP!"

Rumors of wars, of atom bombs falling,
Lands 'cross the seas for help now are calling.
Truly, there's much that looks appalling,
Yet Jesus has told us: "LOOK UP!"

Though enemy weapons are infernal,
God offers to us glories supernal,
With Christ our Lord we have Life eternal,
And He has said we should "LOOK UP!"

Men of science new things are inventing,
Enemy threats are so unrelenting,
But God's Word is preached; souls are repenting,
While Jesus still calls: "LOOK UP!"

Look up! For Christ is now interceding,
He is our Advocate, ever pleading,
God's grace and help we surely are needing,
And Jesus tells us to "LOOK UP!"

Praise God! The coming of Christ is nearing,
He's coming for those who love His appearing.
What a message of comfort, and so cheering!
Let us heed His words and "LOOK UP!"

Thank God for the Light above us shining,
True faith in God keeps us from repining.
For all the trials are for our refining.
Praise God for Christ's message: "LOOK UP!"

—Florence L. Personeus
Written December 1958

LOOKING FOR JESUS

Oh, wonderful, wonderful Jesus,
The Savior who walked on the sea,
Who died for our sins upon Calvary
And lives now that we may be free.

He's coming again in great glory,
And then His dear face we'll behold
And dwell in that beautiful city,
Whose glories can never be told.

Then let us watch and be faithful
Until this journey is o'er,
That we may hear Him say, "Well done,"
On Heaven's glorious shore.

—Florence L. Personeus

JUST A SMILE

It was only a smile and a wave of the hand,
As the giver hastened away,
But it cheered and brightened a heart that was sad
At the close of a weary day.

A smile often comes like a ray of sunlight
Sent from Heaven to us here below;
'Twill bring joy in return, to scatter bright smiles,
For we reap whatever we sow.

If we only knew how a little smile
Might cheer the heart of another,
How it strengthens them to struggle on,
We would smile just to help each other.

For those bright, cheery smiles that come and go
Flash sunshine on Life's thorny way,
And the good they can do not one of us know,
So let's scatter smiles every day.

—Florence L. Personeus

SCHOOL DAYS OF LIFE

Life is a school for everyone:
Lessons to learn, not just have fun.
The Law—a schoolmaster so stern—
Has shown us things that we should learn.
Then the Holy Spirit lights the way,
Instructing us from day to day.

Our Teacher, so patient and so kind,
Wants each lesson learned just right, we find,
Nothing slipped by nor just neglected—
Christ said our best work is expected.
If the Heavenly prize be fairly won,
We must strive till school days here are done.

We shall not regret the training days
If we learn each day to sing God's praise.
We will be thankful for the lessons learned
That from the world our hearts were turned,
Glad that we followed God's dear Son,
When our school days are all done.

Glad we have studied God's Holy Word—
Have learned to use the Spirit's sword,
To stand in faith and help a brother,
So praise our God and lift another,
Have passed the test, the prize have won,
To hear God say to thee, "Well done."

—Florence L. Personeus

WHEN YOU HAVE JESUS

Life is not a disappointment
When you've Jesus in your soul.
He gives peace and consolation,
While the storms around you roll.
He gives grace and dauntless courage,
Strength to bear the heavy load,
And He whispers, "I am with you,"
All along life's weary road.

Though the way be rough and thorny,
Not one trial is for naught.
If you go through trials with Jesus,
Some sweet lesson will be taught.
He doth bear afflictions with you,
Feels your every grief and pain.
Those who suffer here with Jesus,
Someday with Him they shall reign.

People often disappoint us,
Fail to understand or care.
Then what joy to hear Christ whisper,
"Cast on Me your every care."
How can life be sad and lonely
When you've Jesus in your soul?
His great love doth never waver,
While the endless ages roll.

Jesus calms the troubled waters,
Softly whispers, "Peace, be still,"
And the blessed Holy Spirit
Every aching void can fill.
Although life has vexing problems
And so far from our control,
Life is not a disappointment,
When you've Jesus in your soul.

—Florence L. Personeus

THE ALABASTER BOX

(See Mark 14:3-9)
(To the Tune of "No One Ever Cared for Me Like Jesus")

Have you brought your alabaster box to Jesus?
Given Him its treasured perfume, sweet and rare?
Brought to Him your deepest love and heart's devotion,
Bringing comfort to His heart so filled with care?

Chorus:
Jesus loves you with a love unfailing,
Left the glory of His home above,
Came and suffered on the cruel Cross to save you
And reveal God's wondrous love.

Mary's alabaster box so very precious
Brought sweet joy and comfort to His weary soul.
Is your life and love poured out in full surrender?
Are you yielding everything to His control?

Every sacrifice that's made in love to Jesus
Brings a joy to Him, yet not to Him alone,
'Tis recorded in the records up in Heaven,
When rewards are given, then 'twill all be known.

Jesus was the Father's gift so very precious,
Given to redeem this sinful world below,
On the Cross God's alabaster box was broken
That the sweetness of its perfume we might know.

Though the world may say His life was only wasted
When He died upon the Cross of Calvary,
It was only through His death we have salvation
And the pow'r to live a life of victory.

And your friends may say your life is only wasted
If God sends you to the lands beyond the sea.
You will find it pays to follow Jesus always,
He, who said, "Take up your cross and follow Me."

Have you brought your alabaster box to Jesus?
Can He say of you that you've done all you could?
That your life is doing good for Him and others,
Bringing blessing everywhere that Jesus would?

—Florence L. Personeus

LORD, BE THOU OUR GUIDE

Precious Jesus, we would ask Thee,
Be Thou our guide while we are here.
Lead us by the Holy Spirit,
Let us feel Thy presence near.

We have started on a voyage
From this world to one above.
Come, I pray Thee, be our Pilot,
Guide us homeward by Thy love.

Though the storms do overtake us,
Grant that our frail ship may stand
Strong against the world's temptations,
Bring us safely to Thy land.

We must meet temptations many
That would leave us sin-defiled,
But God's Son has come to save us,
So we each may be His child.

Oh, what wonderful redemption!
More than we could ask or think,
Jesus shed His life-blood for us,
Saves us from the awful brink.

Let us serve Thee, blessed Savior,
With our body, mind, and soul,
Then to be forever with Thee,
While the endless ages roll.

—Florence L. Personeus

FAITH IN HIS BLOOD

(See Romans 3:25 & Revelation 12:11)

Under the Blood! 'Tis our mercy seat,
Under the Blood! What a blest retreat!
Under the Blood! There is rest complete
Under the Blood of the Lamb!

Under the Blood! No fear need I know,
Under the Blood! In joy or in woe,
Under the Blood! While onward I go,
Under the Blood of the Lamb!

Under the Blood! When dark grow the skies,
Under the Blood! Tho' storm clouds arise.
Under the Blood! My soul gladly cries,
I'm under the Blood of the Lamb!

Under the Blood! 'Tis there I would hide,
Under the Blood! Whate'er may betide,
Under the Blood! Oh, let me abide
Under the Blood of the Lamb!

Under the Blood! My safe hiding place,
Under the Blood! His love I can trace,
Under the Blood! Till I look on His face,
Under the Blood of the Lamb!

—Florence L. Personeus

TRAVELING ON THE HIGHWAY

(NOTE: When we drove across the United States, as we entered each
state, we obtained a good roadmap. We soon learned the red lines
indicated the best roads to travel. So, in life, Christ shows the best way
with His precious Blood. See 1 Peter 1:18-21.)

(To the tune of "Life's Railway to Heaven")

As you travel on Life's Highway,
From the cradle to the grave,
You will need a roadmap with you
And a Savior, who can save.
God has given us the Bible,
It's directions all are true.
Take the red line of Redemption,
On the Cross Christ died for you.

Refrain:
Come and travel on this highway
To the promised Home above.
Jesus made this road so perfect,
And He paved it with His love.

On this highway of Redemption
There is scenery ever new.
Study faithfully your roadmap,
It will tell you what to do—
How to reach the fair, green pastures
And the waters crystal pure,
Oh, the joy and sweet refreshing,
Although trials we endure.

You may have to cross some desert,
Where the parching, hot winds blow,
Or ascend some rugged mountain,
Feel the chill of some plateau.
But with Jesus close beside you,
There are joys along the way,
Precious promises He whispers,
All along this great highway.

Mind the traffic lights and "Stop" signs,
Always heed the Spirit's voice.
He would guard you from all danger,
Make your heart always rejoice.
Then move forward at His bidding,
He will guide you in all truth
On this highway of Redemption,
For the aged and for the youth.

When the mountains rise before you,
There's a road that's leading through.
If you climb the heights with Jesus,
You will have a glorious view.
Though the road goes through the valleys,
And perhaps the way seems dark,
Keep the scarlet line with Jesus,
Till for Glory we embark.

—Florence L. Personeus

CATCH THE VISION

Catch the vision of Christ the Savior,
As He comes from Jordan's stream,
With the anointing of the Spirit.
See the Dove in radiant gleam!
"Behold the Lamb of God!" John crieth,
"Who taketh away the sin of the world."
He is the Father's Son beloved,
Let His glorious banner be unfurled.

Catch the vision of the lovely Jesus,
As He walks by Galilee,
Seeking out the poor and needy,
Calling, "Come and follow Me."
See Him heal the sick and dying,
Taking children in His arms,
Hushing tempest's raging billows,
Shielding from earth's dread alarms.

Catch the vision of Christ the Savior,
As He hangs on Calvary's tree.
The bleeding, suffering Sacrifice,
Dying there for you and me.
Bearing death's agony and shame,
While people jeer and scream,
"He saved others, now He's dying."
Catch the vision of Love supreme.

Behold! Christ from the grave is risen,
With mighty triumph o'er death and sin!
O, catch the vision of the Redeemer
Telling you lost souls to win.
Go ye quickly to every nation,
Tell them Christ can meet each need.
PRAY! GIVE! GO! O, catch the vision,
Souls are dying. To His Word give heed.

Dear Lord, give us a greater vision,
Anoint with power from on high;
Without a vision, the people perish.
Enlarge our vision, to Thee we cry.
Stir us and give us Thy great compassion
And fervent love, Thy will to learn.
Help us, Lord, to catch the vision
Of whitened fields and Thy soon return.

—Florence L. Personeus

THE CALL FOR REAPERS

Lift up your eyes, and look on the fields,
O reapers, chosen of God (John 4:35),
The harvest is great and waiting for thee.
Are your feet with the Gospel shod?
Jesus is calling for reapers today,
To gather the ripened grain;
There are precious souls, who have gone astray,
Groping in darkness and pain.

Long have the fields been waiting for thee
To harvest the golden sheaves.
Others have toiled and planted seed.
Now there's grain among the leaves.
Prayers have ascended for many a soul,
And they've felt the warmth of God's love,
Which quickened the seed and made it grow
For God's wondrous garners above.

Oh, why has the grain been left so long?
Some was ripened long ago
And some has fallen—beaten down by storms,
Because some reaper failed to go.
Souls are struggling 'mid darkness and sin,
Groping around for the Light,
Waiting for someone to gather them in
Ere comes eternity's night.

The harvest is great, and the laborers few,
Cried Jesus so long ago.
And today He is calling for reapers true
To gather where others did sow.
Oh, pray ye the Lord of the harvest,
That reapers may be sent forth (Luke 10:2)
To gather the souls—far from Jesus—
In the East, West, South and North.

Lift up your eyes and look on the fields,
For they are whitened today,
Ready for you to garner the sheaves.
Oh, hasten, labor, and pray.
Soon will the time of reaping be o'er,
The harvest then will be past;
They cry: "Summer is ended—we are not saved,"
Judgment has come at last (Jeremiah 8:20).

Far and near the fields are bending
With a wealth of ripened grain,
Waiting for the coming reapers
To proclaim that Christ was slain.
Is your heart prepared and ready
With God's Word to prove the truth
Unto all you may encounter,
Both the aged and the youth?

Then be not weary in well doing (Galatians 6:9)
Ye shall reap, if you do not faint,
So, be strong and of good courage,
Without a murmur or complaint.
When our Savior comes from Glory,
Like the rising of the sun,
May each reaper hear Him saying,
"Well done, good and faithful one."

—Florence L. Personeus

AMBASSADORS FOR CHRIST

When God saw the sin and sorrows,
All the troubles mankind was in,
His heart was filled with great compassion,
God sent His Son to die for sin.
Christ came from realms of Glory,
As a baby to Bethlehem,
Became a man, O matchless story!
He humbled Himself to die for them.

He did not come for just a few—
For the good and the kind and true.
Christ came that He might die for all
Who accept Him: He died for you.
Christ died for all and rose again,
Now, He liveth to intercede
At God's right hand in Heav'n above,
Our Advocate for us to plead.

Christ died for ALL, so live for Him,
For we have been bought with a price.
We're not our own to live for self,
But for Christ, a live sacrifice.
All that we have, and all we are
Has been given to us by God.
Let us spread the Gospel near and far,
As we walk this earthly sod.

Christ for all, and all for Christ,
May this ever our motto be;
Serving the Lord with all our hearts
Till His blessed face we see.
Ambassadors for Christ are we,
To represent our Savior-King,
Who died that we might be set free.
Let us His praises ever sing.

—Florence L. Personeus

PETER THE FISHERMAN

Out in a fishing boat, bold and strong,
Peter the fisherman toiled hard and long.
Day after day, in sunshine and storm,
Even at night his rugged form
Threw out the nets and dragged them in.
A rough, cursing fisherman, full of sin,
Until one day he chanced to see
A Stranger on the shores of Galilee,
A Man with a face so kind, yet strong,
So different from the common throng.

"Have you no fish?" Peter heard Him ask.
"None. Been fishing all night. What a task!"
Then into his boat the Stranger came,
A Nazareth carpenter, Jesus by name.
"Launch out in the deep, and you will find."
Peter doubted His words, but His tone was kind.
The nets were dropped from out the boat,
And now they could scarcely keep afloat.
Such a load of fish Peter never had seen,
But the Presence of Jesus made him feel unclean.

When they got to shore, Peter fell at His feet.
"I'm a sinful man and completely beat."
"Come, follow Me," Jesus said to him then,
"And I will make you a fisher of men."
Peter left his boat and the fishing nets
And his life of sin, with its daily frets.
He saw mighty miracles Jesus wrought;
He heard wonderful truths by Jesus taught.
Thousands were fed with five loaves of bread.
Jesus healed the sick and raised the dead.

Many days and months the same paths they trod,
Until Peter cried, "Thou art the Son of God.
New faith and hope Your message brings,
For none but God could do such things."
Then came that night of awful shame
When wicked men to the Garden came.
Would Peter ever forget that sight,
When they led Christ away that dreadful night?
And in fear and doubt he had Christ denied
As the mob yelled, "Let Him be crucified!"

Peter saw Him nailed to the cruel Cross.
What anguish he felt at the awful loss.
His heart was crushed by deep despair.
Christ in a tomb! They left Him there.
But Easter morn, strange news he heard.
Could he believe the wondrous word?
"Christ is living!" Mary said 'twas true.
"Tell My disciples, and Peter too."
Then he knelt once again at Jesus' side,
"Thou knowest I love thee, dear Lord," he cried.

Then "Feed My lambs and My sheep," Christ said.
"Tell them I have risen from the dead.
But tarry ye in Jerusalem
Till ye have power to witness to them."
Ten days Peter waited and watched and prayed.
The Holy Spirit came and with them stayed.
Then Peter rose and preached with power,
A different man from that same hour.

—Florence L. Personeus

MOTHER'S BIG TASK

God gave mothers a wonderful task:
　　Teaching children of His love,
　　Training them to pray, and ask
　　How to reach the Home above.

Jesus was glad when mothers came,
　　Bringing their children to Him.
　　He lifted them up in His arms;
　　Joy filled their hearts to the brim.

　　Jesus is just the same today,
　　With tender love for everyone,
He wants to hear the mothers pray,
And children too, when day is done.

　　Oh, mothers have the biggest job
　　That anyone on earth can find:
　　The job of training souls for God,
　　,And always to be good and kind.

　　　　　　　　—Florence L. Personeus

A MOTHER'S PRAYER

A boy was standing at life's crossroads.
"Which way shall I take?" said he.
He thought of his mother and her prayers,
But he said, "I want to be free."

He went his way in the paths of sin,
Forgetting his mother's prayer.
He did not seem like the boy he'd been;
To go home, he did not dare.

But Mother did not forget her boy,
Though he wandered far and wild.
She pleaded for him each day in prayer,
"Lord Jesus, please save my child."

Her boy said, "I want to be free."
And he took the downward road.
He found himself in a prison cell,
Crushed beneath sin's heavy load.

He thought of his mother's anguished prayers.
He longed for her tender love.
Could she forgive all the pain he'd caused?
Would God forgive him above?

He knelt on the hard, cold floor and prayed,
"Oh, God, will You cleanse my soul?
Forgive and help me to live for Thee,
Oh, save me and make me whole."

Far away, his mother knelt in prayer,
"Oh where is my boy tonight?
My Father, I've placed him in Your care,
Lord, help him to do the right."

It was Mother's Day; a letter came
From a city far away.
"Dear Mother, the Lord has saved my soul.
I'm happy in Him today."

"Yes, your loving prayers have followed me,
No matter how far I'd roam.
Sin brought me sorrow and misery,
But now I'm coming home."

What a joyous cry burst from her heart,
As she knelt beside her chair:
"Thank You, dear Lord, how faithful Thou art.
Thank You for answering prayer."

—Florence L. Personeus

THANKSGIVING DAY

"O, give thanks unto the Lord,
For His goodness endures forever."
Thank Him for each morning's dawn;
His love doth fail us never.
Thank Him for His presence daily,
Guiding, guarding us each hour,
Giving us new strength and wisdom,
As we trust the Spirit's power.

Thank God for the sunshine bright,
And for the days so dark and gray;
Thank Him for the winter's snow,
And thank Him when it goes away.
Life has its trials as well as joys,
But we are thankful for the rain.
Jesus says, "Lo, I am with you,"
As He soothes and heals our pain.

Thank the Lord for His blessings
So abundant and free each day,.
More than we can ever number,
And more than what we even pray.
O, give thanks for Christ our Savior,
Who came to earth to set us free;
He bore our sins and died to save us
In agony on Calvary.

O, give thanks, Christ rose victorious;
And now He lives forevermore
To help us when we call upon Him
And guides us on toward Heaven's shore.
Thank God we have the Holy Bible
To teach us what we ought to do.
Thank Him for every precious promise
That gives us faith and courage too.

Thank God, we have a blessed hope:
Our Lord will soon return again
And claim all those who look for Him,
That they may live and with Him reign.
Time is short; we must be ready.
Strive to win some souls today.
Tell them of the love of Jesus;
Point them to the Narrow Way.

Oh, thank the Lord when you awaken,
And give Him praise all through the day.
"Remember all His benefits"
And Jesus' words to "watch and pray."
"His mercies are new every morning,"
So, each day is Thanksgiving Day.

—Florence L. Personeus

CHRISTMAS GREETINGS

'Tis Christmas again, and greetings we send
All over the country, to every dear friend,
Because we desire again to remind you
That you're not forgotten, where'er this may find you.

And let us remember the Savior who came,
That to humble shepherds did angels proclaim,
"Behold, good tidings of great joy, I bring,
For unto you is born Christ, the Lord," the King.

And this great glad message is for all
Who come repenting and on Jesus call.
He will gladly pardon, cleanse, and forgive,
That with Him in glory we may ever live.

Christ is the Light of the World, we see,
And He alone can make people free.
Jesus will help us each victory to win,
For He came to save His people from sin.

Rejoice! Because this message still is true,
Christ was born, and died for everyone—for you.
And soon He is coming to claim His bride;
Pray always to be worthy to stand by His side.

"Great joy shall be to all people," the message rang,
And "Glory to God in the highest," the angels sang.
This message of good tidings is for you today;
Christ gives us a peace that does not pass away.

—Florence L. Personeus

CHRISTMAS FAR FROM HOME

'Tis Christmas again, and I'm thinking
Of this war-wracked world of ours,
Of the homes that are broken and bleeding,
Of the graves not strewn with flow'rs,
Of brave young lives, far from home and dear ones,
Scattered over land and sea,
Far from home and its joys and its comforts,
Striving to make the world free.

Brave men in Coast Guard, Army, and Navy
Are thinking of those at home,
With a wistful gaze at some photo dear,
As they view the ocean's foam.
Brave mothers and wives and other loved ones
Are thinking of dear ones too,
Breathing a prayer for those far away now,
The men in khaki and blue.

Christmas! And many are far from home,
Some not in uniform clad,
Also missionaries in foreign lands,
True and brave as any lad.
Thinking of home and loved ones too,
They left for the Master's sake,
While they tell of Christ, who left His Home,
That the pow'r of sin He'd break.

When Joseph and Mary reached Bethlehem,
They too were far from home,
With their only shelter a stable dim,
Not near the temple's dome.
For in Bethlehem, the prophet wrote,
The Ruler of Israel should come,
Like a lamb to the slaughter to be led,
As a sheep before shearers is dumb.

The Savior was far from Home,
When rejected by the sons of men.
And He understands the lonely heart
Better than told by word or pen.
Christ left His glorious Home in Heav'n,
To be born of a Virgin, we see,
And He is the great Immanuel,
Who alone makes us truly free.

Though scattered far from home and friends,
Christ is the Friend who is always near
And ready to comfort everyone
Who will accept His love and cheer.
He knows what it's like to yearn for home,
To be tempted and weary and sad,
But He's made the way to Heav'n above,
So our hearts might ever be glad.

Then let us be thankful that Jesus came
From His Home in Glory above.
Let Him fill the lonely place in your life
And reveal God's wonderful love.
It may not be so very long
Until Jesus shall reign as King,
And we shall join the happy song
The redeemed of this earth shall sing.

—Florence L. Personeus

THE NEW YEAR

Lo! A New Year before me now stands.
I trustingly leave it, O Christ, in Thy hands.
Thou seest and knowest the enemy's snares,
The trials and testings, the burdens and cares.
'Tis well that from me all these things are hid,
Only help me, Lord Jesus, to do what You bid.
Thou very well knowest there's no good in me,
But sweet falls Thy whisper, "I'll never leave thee."

Tho' Satan may bluster, your faith try to shake,
Remember I've promised, "I'll never forsake."
So blest is Thy promise, so faithful and sure,
Then help me, dear Jesus, to bravely endure
Whatever the trial, whatever the test,
Knowing that always Thy way is best.
Then looking to Thee, I will banish my fear,
And trust Thee to guide me all through this New Year.

—Florence L. Personeus

GOD-SPEED TO THE CHALLENGERS

Go forth to the conflict, ye Challengers,
In the battle against wrong and sin.
The hosts of evil are sweeping the land
With self, a subtle foe within.
Christ, our mighty Captain, calls on you to go,
Preaching His great salvation true
To everybody in this world below,
Not only preach it, but LIVE it too.

Three years you've been in this Armory grand,
Where you've buckled the armor on,
Fitting and proving each needed piece,
That the victory might be won.
Hold fast your helmet of Salvation sure,
When fragments of doubt and fears assail;
Keep heart and thoughts all clean and pure
Through Jesus' Blood, if you'd prevail.

The breastplate of His Righteousness
Must guard your heart and life each day,
And as you challenge the hosts of sin,
There's victory when you watch and pray.
The girdle of Truth is Christ the Lord,
He is the Way, the Truth, the Life,
The great Almighty, Living Word,
Can make you victors in every strife.

The road to Heaven is never smooth,
The struggles with Satan do not cease,
But your feet can walk upon that road
When shod with the Gospel of Peace.
The shield of Faith can quench each dart
That the devil shoots your way.
The Bible is the sword to wield
For victory in every fray.

235

As soldiers you must meet the foe
And remember, the battle is real.
The lessons learned will help, we know,
May your courage be as true as steel.
When you say farewell to N. B. I.
And the friends and teachers here,
You may not know where your work will be,
And the future may not be clear.

But Jesus said when He sends His sheep
That He always goes before
To clear the path He would have you keep
And open for you His door.
There's many a foe would block your path,
And you can challenge the same
And push ahead in the Master's cause,
To conquer in Jesus' name.

Some may go east, and others go west,
And some to the south or north
To carry the blessed Gospel truth
Whenever Christ says, "Go forth!"
O, tell the whole world Christ died for all
To redeem and cleanse from sin,
To give power to overcome
When His Spirit dwells within.

Tho' scattered far in the Master's field,
We may never meet here any more,
But let us be faithful to our Lord,
So we'll meet on Heaven's fair shore.
God grant we may hear Christ say, "Well done,"
When we bow in His presence sweet,
So, let us toil that when Jesus comes,
We'll have sheaves to lay at His feet.

—Written for Dorothy White when she graduated from
Northwest Bible Institute in Seattle in 1945
By Florence L. Personeus

WINTER

Although the storms blow around us,
And the snow falls so white and deep,
God gives peace and joy within us,
For our Shepherd guards His sheep.
His dear presence sweetly thrills us,
Fills our hearts with joyful song.
The Holy Spirit warms and fills us
With trustful hope and courage strong.

—Florence L. Personeus

ABOUT THE AUTHOR

The author, AnnaLee (Cousart) Conti, granddaughter of Carl and Florence Personeus, is a fifth generation ordained minister of the Gospel in the Personeus family. AnnaLee grew up in Alaska and met her husband, Bob, while they were students at the University of Alaska, Fairbanks. They have pastored in New York State for twenty-five years, including pioneering a church. They have a son and four grandchildren.

AnnaLee (B.A., University of Alaska; M.A., Assemblies of God Theological Seminary) has for years written church school curriculum and freelance articles published in magazines, including *The Pentecostal Evangel* and *Woman's Touch*. She also teaches GED and adult basic education classes, in addition to adult Bible classes in her church.

Printed in the United States
778900003B

9 780759 688995